W9-ABK-901

people in the NEWS

Dwayne Johnson

by Sheila Wyborny

South Huntington Pub. Lib.
145 Pidgeon Hill Rd.
Huntington Sta., N.Y. 11746

LUCENT BOOKS
A part of Gale, Cengage Learning

GALE
CENGAGE Learning™

Detroit • New York • San Francisco • New Haven, Conn • Waterville, Maine • London

GALE
CENGAGE Learning

LIBRARY OF CONGRESS CATALOGING-IN-PUBLICATION DATA

Wyborny, Sheila, 1950-
  Dwayne Johnson / by Sheila Wyborny.
    p. cm. — (People in the news)
  Includes bibliographical references and index.
  ISBN 978-1-4205-0125-4 (hardcover)
  1. Rock (Wrestler)—Juvenile literature. 2. Wrestlers—United States—Biography—Juvenile literature. 3. Actors—United States—Biography—Juvenile literature. I. Title.
  GV1196.R63W93 2009
  796.812092—dc22
  [B]
                                                          2008050900

Lucent Books
27500 Drake Rd.
Farmington Hills, MI 48331

ISBN-13: 978-1-4205-0125-4
ISBN-10: 1-4205-0125-9

Contents

Foreword   **4**

Introduction   **6**
Successes and Challenges

Chapter 1   **10**
A Royal Family and Rocky Roads

Chapter 2   **29**
Joining the Family Business

Chapter 3   **46**
Making His Name

Chapter 4   **61**
Introducing the Rock

Chapter 5   **77**
Knowing Your Roles

Notes   **92**

Important Dates   **94**

For More Information   **96**

Index   **99**

Picture Credits   **103**

About the Author   **104**

Fame and celebrity are alluring. People are drawn to those who walk in fame's spotlight, whether they are known for great accomplishments or for notorious deeds. The lives of the famous pique public interest and attract attention, perhaps because their experiences seem in some ways so different from, yet in other ways so similar to, our own.

Newspapers, magazines, and television regularly capitalize on this fascination with celebrity by running profiles of famous people. For example, television programs such as *Entertainment Tonight* devote all of their programming to stories about entertainment and entertainers. Magazines such as *People* fill their pages with stories of the private lives of famous people. Even newspapers, newsmagazines, and television news frequently delve into the lives of well-known personalities. Despite the number of articles and programs, few provide more than a superficial glimpse at their subjects.

Lucent's People in the News series offers young readers a deeper look into the lives of today's newsmakers, the influences that have shaped them, and the impact they have had in their fields of endeavor and on other people's lives. The subjects of the series hail from many disciplines and walks of life. They include authors, musicians, athletes, political leaders, entertainers, entrepreneurs, and others who have made a mark on modern life and who, in many cases, will continue to do so for years to come.

These biographies are more than factual chronicles. Each book emphasizes the contributions, accomplishments, or deeds that have brought fame or notoriety to the individual and shows how that person has influenced modern life. Authors portray their subjects in a realistic, unsentimental light. For example, Bill Gates—the cofounder and chief executive officer of the software giant Microsoft—has been instrumental in making personal computers the most vital tool of the modern age. Few dispute his business savvy, his perseverance, or his technical expertise, yet critics say he is ruthless in his dealings with competitors and driven more by his desire to maintain Microsoft's dominance in the computer industry than by an interest in furthering technology.

In these books, young readers will encounter inspiring stories about real people who achieved success despite enormous obstacles. Oprah Winfrey—the most powerful, most watched, and wealthiest woman on television today—spent the first six years of her life in the care of her grandparents while her unwed mother sought work and a better life elsewhere. Her adolescence was colored by promiscuity, pregnancy at age fourteen, rape, and sexual abuse.

Each author documents and supports his or her work with an array of primary and secondary source quotations taken from diaries, letters, speeches, and interviews. All quotes are footnoted to show readers exactly how and where biographers derive their information and provide guidance for further research. The quotations enliven the text by giving readers eyewitness views of the life and accomplishments of each person covered in the People in the News series.

In addition, each book in the series includes photographs, annotated bibliographies, timelines, and comprehensive indexes. For both the casual reader and the student researcher, the People in the News series offers insight into the lives of today's newsmakers—people who shape the way we live, work, and play in the modern age.

Successes and Challenges

Dwayne Johnson's life has been anything but dull and average. Still only in his thirties, Johnson has already had three careers: football, wrestling, and acting. His childhood was not typical, either. The son of an African American wrestling champion and grandson of the leader of a Samoan wrestling dynasty, Johnson and his family moved frequently as his father followed wrestling jobs. Young Dwayne was always the new kid in school, and usually the biggest kid in the class. This frequently led to confrontations as other boys sought to prove their masculinity by picking fights with Dwayne. With a tall body and a short temper, he seldom walked away from a fight.

Athletic Potential

Once in high school, Johnson discovered his talent for football. He learned to channel his temper into more positive action on the football field, where he played well enough to attract the attention of college recruiters. After a disappointing start, he had a successful college football career with the University of Miami before enduring the disappointment of being overlooked by the NFL (National Football League). After one dismal and brief season with a Canadian football team as a practice player, living in a fleabag apartment with several other men and sleeping on mattresses salvaged from dumpsters, Johnson returned to Florida and began training in the family business, professional wrestling.

Although wrestling was literally in his blood, Johnson did not simply walk into the ring and take up the career; he had to train and train hard. He became more familiar with the moves and the vocabulary of professional wrestling he had learned as a child. Growing up in the business, Johnson had always known that professional wrestling is about carefully planned choreography and a certain amount of showmanship, rather than actual competition. He learned the skills from his father and practiced the skills he learned in the equivalent of the minor leagues, performing in cattle barns, car lots, and wherever else the matches were arranged. This is where he began to develop the performance skills that attract wrestling fans and inspire their love/hate relationship with the sport of wrestling. They love the action and enjoy hurling insults at the hated villains, the bad guys.

The World of Wrestling

Johnson's formal WWF (World Wrestling Federation) debut took place in Madison Square Garden in New York City before a huge crowd of wrestling fans as well as a large pay-per-view audience. However, his "baby-face" or good-guy image did not inspire a big response from the fans that night. At best his welcome to the WWF was lukewarm. Over time he discovered that he could not get the kind of fan reaction he wanted from being good guy Rocky Maivia, so he changed his character and became the Rock, an arrogant, in-your-face, generally insulting bad guy that could bring out strong feelings in the fans. As the Rock, Johnson developed a number of catch phrases that the fans began to identify with him. The big, brash, bold wrestler caught on in a big way.

By the time Dwayne Johnson became the Rock, the best professional wrestlers were no longer scrimping financially to get by. The top professionals were earning large sums of money from product endorsements and commercials to add to their income from the ring. The Rock took full advantage of his opportunities and was soon living in a home many times larger than his early slum efficiency apartments.

The Price of Fame

However, fame comes with a price. Johnson soon learned that he and his wife Dany would have to sacrifice much of their privacy for the trappings of stardom. Whenever they were in a public place, fans would stop them, seeking autographs and asking to have their photographs taken with the Rock. Sometimes the Johnsons were surrounded with mobs of people pushing, shoving, and demanding their moment with their favorite wrestling star. Johnson had long since learned his lesson about the dangers of giving in to a short temper, though, and was often more courteous to the wrestling fans than they were to him and his wife. He was especially patient and courteous with his youngest fans. No matter how busy or tired Johnson was, if children approached him, he made time for them.

New Opportunities

After several years in the WWF ring, acting opportunities began to come his way, and Johnson was not a man to turn down an opportunity. Unlike a number of other sports figures who decided to take a stab at the movies, playing a few forgettable roles and discovering they had no acting talent, Johnson found that he had a natural flare for the screen. After a few television roles, including hosting the popular program *Saturday Night Live*, and acting roles, including the lead in *The Scorpion King*, Johnson decided it was time to stop bouncing between the wrestling ring and acting roles, and he became a full-time actor. He also laid aside his ring persona—the brash, aggressive character of the Rock. In a number of interviews, he asked that his fans start calling him by his name, Dwayne Johnson.

Although Johnson will always be remembered for wrestling as the Rock, he has now been acting for almost as many years as he spent in the ring. When he is not acting, he is often involved in charity work, such as educational programs for disadvantaged youth and disaster relief efforts. He has been the National Afterschool spokesman, and in 2006 Johnson and his wife made their first donation, $2 million, to the University of Miami.

Though now divorced from his wife, the two share a daughter, Simone Alexandra, and maintain a friendly relationship. In the meantime Johnson enjoys his time with his daughter, continues his involvement in various charities, and has a string of movie roles planned far into the future.

Chapter 1

A Royal Family and Rocky Roads

Being born into a family business is no guarantee that a child will or should one day join that business. Such was the case for young Dwayne Johnson. As a child, he frequently moved with his family from place to place, following his father's career as a professional wrestler. Dwayne regularly watched from ringside as his father, Rocky Johnson, tossed opponents from the ring and sometimes got tossed himself. When Dwayne briefly checked out his school's wrestling team, though, he found school wrestling matches dull and boring in comparison to the stylized acrobatics of the professional ring. In fact, for many years after the young teenager spent that brief time with the school's wrestling team, he thought his professional career would be football. However, injuries and a series of bad experiences cut that dream short. As his pursuit of professional football ended, though, a new path emerged. A decade after walking away from the school wrestling team, Dwayne Johnson entered the ring once again; this time as a professional wrestler, a third-generation member of the family business, professional wrestling.

A Royal Samoan Family of Wrestling

Dwayne Johnson's wrestling lineage began with his grandfather Fanene Leifi Pita Maivia, known as "High Chief" Peter Maivia. Maivia was born in western Samoa in the 1930s. "High Chief" was not just

Dwayne Johnson's wrestling lineage began with his grandfather Fanene Maivia, who was descended from a royal Samoan family.

his performing name, though, and Maivia was not just royalty in the wrestling business. Maivia was descended from a royal Samoan family and was the elected chief of his clan. And Maivia conducted himself with the dignity befitting a member of a royal family. Throughout his life Maivia was well-respected among the wrestling community as well as by the people of Pacific cultures.

The Samoan Culture

Most fans know that Dwayne Johnson's father is African Canadian and his mother is Samoan. Johnson has always taken pride in the heritage of each of his parents. However, many people know little about the Samoan culture.

Samoa is a group of six islands in the South Pacific, about 2,400 miles (3,862km) southwest of Hawaii. Said to be Polynesia's oldest culture, Samoans have occupied these islands for three thousand years. *Samoa* means sacred earth. To the Samoan people, this island group is a sacred place and they protect and cherish it.

Their system of government is called *fa'amatai*. The *matai*, or chief, governs the *aiga*, or extended family. The members of the aiga respect their chief and revere their elders. They are generous toward one another and take the same care of the children of other adults in their group as they do their own. They believe their extended families should work together and be mutually supportive for the common good.

Samoans are known for their handcrafted products, such as kava bowls. These are round wooden bowls of a variety of sizes with stubby legs on the bottom. Another Samoan craft is called *siapo*. Siapo are pictures or patterns painted on mulberry bark that has been hammered into sheets.

Samoan crafts, traditional music and dance, and system of government have been handed down through generations. The Samoans are a proud people who respect and honor the culture handed down by their ancestors and work diligently to keep it alive.

As a young man, though, the 5-foot, 9-inch young Samoan (1.75m), weighing 240 pounds (109kg), attracted the attention of New Zealand wrestling promoters, not because he was of royal blood but because of his size. Young Maivia moved to New Zealand, where he began his training as a wrestler. He also spent some time training in London, England, a place that seemed very exotic to the young Samoan. However, the first years of his professional career were spent in New Zealand. Maivia proved to be a natural. In August 1964, less than a year into his professional career, he won the New Zealand Heavyweight title from Steve Rickard in Auckland. Victory was brief, however, when just three days later Rickard defeated Maivia and regained the championship. Maivia had acquired a taste for victory, however, and he won the NWA Australasian Heavyweight title the next year, in 1965, a title he held until 1968. As they are today, matches were also scripted in those days, but most fans did not know it.

While living in New Zealand, Maivia met his future wife Lia. After the couple married, they had a daughter, Ata, and two sons, Peter Fanene Jr. and Toa. Maivia won many more championships in New Zealand before he, his wife, and his children moved to Hawaii, where Maivia wrestled a number of years. The family's next move was to San Francisco, California, at the beginning of the 1970s.

While in California the Maivias met another Samoan family, the Anoa'is, Tovale and Amituanai. In true Samoan tradition the two families "adopted" each other, and the men in the families became like blood brothers, making no distinction between who was related by birth and who was related by this bond. The Anoa'i children became Maivia's nephews, a family link that would continue throughout Maivia's life and would extend through two more generations of his family and the the Anoa'i family.

Soon Maivia dominated the West Coast wrestling region, winning championships in San Francisco and Los Angeles. He excelled as both a single wrestler and a tag team member, pairing up with such legends as Billy White Wolf, Pat Patterson (who would later become a mentor of Maivia's grandson), and Ray "the Crippler" Stevens.

In addition to a successful wrestling career, Maivia worked in the movies for a time. In fact, he played a small role as a villain

Dwayne Johnson poses with his mother Ata in this 2004 photo. Ata married wrestler Rocky Johnson in 1967 and Dwayne was born five years later.

in the 1967 James Bond film *You Only Live Twice*. By then Maivia was also training other wrestlers, so the film's directors made use of his teaching skills, coordinating fight scenes for the movie.

Enter Rocky Johnson

While working in California, Maivia became acquainted with African Canadian wrestler Rocky "Soulman" Johnson. This meeting would prove to be an important one in the lives of both men for both personal and professional reasons. Born Wade Bowles in Nova Scotia in 1944 and raised in Toronto, Johnson drove a truck

It's Not All Fake: A Brief Description of Professional Wrestling

In the United States as well as many other countries, professional wrestling is part entertainment and part sport. The feuds and friction between wrestlers consist of scripted storylines, called angles, and the matches themselves have been carefully planned and choreographed. Many wrestlers who appear to be mortal enemies in the ring are, in fact, actually good friends. After hurling one another around the ring and slinging insults and threats, they may go out to dinner together.

However, the risk of injury is quite real. Wrestlers are carefully trained athletes, and, like any other athletes, despite careful preparations, they are sometimes injured. Dislocated shoulders, torn ligaments, concussions, and other injuries which may require surgery or physical therapy can take them away from their sport for anywhere from a few days to several months.

High-flying wrestlers confront each other in the ring.

to support himself as he began his wrestling training while still a teenager. He made his professional debut at Maple Leaf Gardens in Toronto in 1966. He continued to wrestle in the Toronto area until the winter of 1967, when he moved to the west coast of Canada and teamed with Don Leo Jonathan. In April of that year the two men won the Canadian Tag Team Championship from Chris and John Tolos. He continued to wrestle between Toronto and Vancouver for several years.

Johnson was a seasoned wrestler who had already paid his dues in the professional ring by the time he met Maivia and became one of his tag team partners. Johnson had other fighting experience as well. At one time he had been a sparring partner of boxing champion George Foreman.

Johnson met Maivia's daughter Ata at the taping of one of the wrestling matches. The two soon began dating and fell in love. Maivia disapproved of the relationship and tried to break up the pair. Maivia objected to their relationship because Johnson was a wrestler, and since Maivia was a wrestler himself, he knew how hard a life his daughter would have if she married Johnson. At the time, although professional wrestling was popular entertainment, wrestlers did not make much money, and they had to move frequently. The couple would not be discouraged, though. Since the family objected so strongly to their intended marriage, Ata and Johnson eloped. Because they went against her father's wishes, the young couple was estranged from Ata's family for nearly a year. The relationship improved when their son Dwayne was born. In fact, Johnson was finally accepted as a member of the Maivia wrestling family.

The Soul Patrol

Johnson continued to make a name for himself in the National Wrestling Alliance (NWA) throughout the 1970s, becoming a top contender. He fought against then–world champions Terry Funk and Harley Race. Johnson performed well as a tag team member and was part of several winning teams before being recruited by the World Wrestling Federation (WWF) and paired with Tony Atlas, also a popular black wrestler, in 1983. The duo became known as the Soul Patrol. Ironically, the two defeated Maivia's adopted nephews, tag team champions Afa and Sika Anoa'i, in November 1983, making Johnson and Atlas the first black WWF Tag Team Champions. During his varied career, Johnson wrestled for the NWA as well as the WWF. At times he was also involved in a number of smaller wrestling associations in Europe. He would go on to hold over three dozen wrestling titles during his career.

Purchasing a Wrestling Territory

In the meantime Maivia, his wife, and their two sons moved back to Hawaii in the late 1970s, where he purchased the NWA Polynesian Pro Wrestling territory. After a period of faltering, the Polynesian territory began to thrive and grow under Maivia and his wife's leadership. Though not a wrestler herself, Lia was an active participant in the family business, working as a fight promoter for many years.

Maivia also continued to wrestle in Hawaii and in other parts of the world. By this time he had acquired his tribal tattoos, symbols of his rank, on his torso and legs. His grandson Dwayne Johnson later commented, "My grandfather's massive torso looked to me like a brilliant and vibrant cityscape, with dozens of intersecting lines and angles, each of which told its own little story."[1] However, Maivia had begun backing away from title-winning bouts not long after he purchased the Hawaiian territory from promoter Ed Francis. This was because his primary goal was to promote the wrestling territory rather than himself. He won his final title, defeating Rick Davidson for the NWA Americas title, in Los Angeles in 1981.

During his years in the business, Peter "High Chief" Maivia set a standard in the professional wrestling industry that carries on to the third generation. The family tradition has been upheld by honorary nephews, such as Afa, Sika, and Samu Anoa'i, and Eddie Fatu, known in the ring as Umaga. Other names familiar to wrestling fans include Jimmy Snuka Jr., Rikishi, and Rosey, or Ro'Z, also members of Johnson's grandfather's blood-brother family. The legion of names continues with Maivia's son-in-law Rocky Johnson, Maivia's son Toa, and, of course, his grandson Dwayne "the Rock" Johnson, the son of his daughter Ata and son-in-law Johnson.

The Anoa'i Wrestling Family

Although they are not actually related by blood, the Anoa'i wrestling family and Dwayne Johnson have close personal ties. His grandfather Peter Maivia was a blood brother of the Anoa'i family. The family's founders, Reverend Amituanai and his wife Tovale had four children: sons Afa, Junior, and Sika, and one daughter, Vera. Of the four, only Afa and Sika became wrestlers, a tag team called the Wild Samoans. However, all four of the children had children of their own who became wrestlers. Afa's sons, known in the ring as Samu, Afa Jr., and L.A. Smooth, are all wrestlers. His daughter Monica is the widow of wrestler Gary Albright. Junior is the father of the late wrestler Yokozuna. Sika's oldest son wrestles under the name Ro'Z. Vera married Solofa Fatu and all three of her sons became wrestlers. They are Sam, known as Tama; Solofa Jr. called Rikishi; and Eddie, called Umaga.

Growing Up in the Business

Dwayne Douglas Johnson was born in Hayward, California, on May 2, 1972. He was Rocky and Ata Johnson's first and only child. Dwayne's earliest memories were not typical of a child in the 1970s. Some of his first toys were his father's championship belts, and as a child of five, he would often sit at ringside with his mother while his father wrestled. He later spoke of his early exposure to the world of wrestling: "I grew up in the business, was kept close to the business, and never sheltered from it."[2]

Dwayne was a very active child and prone to mischief. As a small child, at night he would crawl out of his crib to play instead of going to sleep. At the armories and stadiums where his father wrestled, Dwayne would slip away from his mother and go exploring. Not even the family pet escaped his mischief. By the time Dwayne started school, he was using his dog to practice wrestling moves. At this point in his life, though, his parents were sure wrestling was just a game to Dwayne, another way to play and use up some of his extra energy. At least they hoped so.

The wrestling business was hard on families. Some stayed behind while the father traveled the United States to different wrestling territories and matches. However, Rocky Johnson did not want to be separated from his family. He took them with him when he moved from territory to territory. This meant that they moved frequently. In fact, by the time Dwayne was five years old, his family had already moved five times.

For Johnson, preparation for the ring included practices with his dog.

Frequent Moves

Moving around a lot meant that Dwayne was usually the new kid on the block, and after he was old enough to go to school, the new kid in class. As he grew older and larger, other boys often picked fights with him so they could prove how tough they were. Dwayne usually did not start the fights, but he did not back away from them, either. Since he was usually the largest kid on the playground, he won the fights, and sometimes the other boys got hurt. When this happened, Dwayne was branded a bully, even when he was only defending himself. One of these fights was not even a real fight—it was actually a demonstration. One of Dwayne's friends had asked Dwayne to show him some of the wrestling moves he had learned from his father. During the demonstration the boy was injured. Dwayne felt bad about hurting his friend and had not meant to injure him. However, Dwayne was still suspended from school for fighting, which got him into trouble with his mother. She, not his father, was the parent in charge of handing out the discipline.

Despite the frequent moves and getting into trouble for fighting, Dwayne was a good student and made good grades. His parents wanted their son to get a good education so he could have a better life. They made sure he did not miss school, studied for his tests, and kept up with his homework, no matter how much they moved. With good grades, they knew that their son would be able to get into college and have a career that would allow him the opportunity to put down roots somewhere and have a normal home life. But for the rest of their years together as a family, they had to keep moving and following the wrestling jobs.

One of the family's moves took them to Hawaii, where Dwayne was able to spend some time with his grandparents. Now eight years old, Dwayne was old enough to understand what an important man his grandfather was, and that he was respected both inside and outside of the wrestling community. However, his time with his grandfather would be sadly brief. Maivia had worked hard to promote his wrestling territory but had neglected his own health. He refused to go to the doctor when he had obvious warning signs that his health and his life were in jeopardy. By the time

Maivia did go to the doctor, it was too late. Dwayne's grandfather, wrestling legend High Chief Peter Maivia, died from cancer on June 13, 1982. His grandfather's memorial service in Honolulu, Hawaii, attended by thousands of fans and friends, reinforced what Dwayne already knew—that his grandfather had been an important and greatly respected man.

Pro Dreams Meet Harsh Realities

A few years after his grandfather's death, Dwayne's family returned to the mainland, moving this time to Pennsylvania. This particular move worked in Dwayne's favor. While living in Pennsylvania, Dwayne developed a serious interest in football, a good choice for a 6-foot-tall, 170-pound thirteen-year-old (1.8m, 77kg). He worked hard to become a good football player and to keep up with his studies, but he also had other interests, such as girls.

While his mature size and muscular build attracted the attention of football coaches and tough guys spoiling for fights, it also attracted quite a bit of female attention. At fourteen, Dwayne had an eighteen-year-old girlfriend. He admitted later that all of this attention made him cocky and somewhat arrogant: "In my mind, I was God's gift to women . . . the player to end all players . . . the mack of all daddies."[3]

He did not allow his interest in girls to sidetrack him, though, and he became one of the top high school football players in the state of Pennsylvania. During his senior year a number of colleges were scouting him. By the time he graduated from high school, he had been approached by a number of colleges with offers of football scholarships. He later recalled that exciting time:

> It's amazing what a simple letter can do to a kid's ego. You walk to the mailbox and there's an envelope with Penn State or Notre Dame stamped in the upper left-hand corner, and your heart just about does a somersault. Then the phone starts ringing . . . day and night. And then the assistant coaches begin showing up, knocking at your front door after dinner or visiting you at school. It's extraordinarily flattering, and it can really go to your head if you're not careful.[4]

During a University of Miami game, defensive lineman Dwayne Johnson (94) rushes the offense.

Dwayne considered all of the offers and opportunities. Ultimately, he settled on the University of Miami because he respected their recruiting methods. They did not offer him anything under the table, such as cars or money. They just offered him the opportunity to go to college and play football.

Injury and Disappointment

Dwayne arrived in Miami in the summer of 1989, ready to begin football practice. There, he experienced a large dose of culture shock. First, Dwayne had never been away from family and on his own. Second, at the University of Miami, he was not the largest football player or a big star as he had been in high school. Many of the other players were as large as Dwayne, and some were even larger. Also, many of them could play football just as well as he could. Some were even better—a lot better. Dwayne had plenty of work ahead of him during the summer training program if he expected to see time on the field as a freshman. He was willing to work hard and do whatever he had to do to get that opportunity. Finally, toward the end of summer football practice with the first game practically in sight, Dwayne was tackled from behind and taken to the ground during a practice session. He had been tackled many times over the summer, but this time something went wrong. His shoulder was badly injured. The trainers could

The Miami Hurricanes

Dwayne Johnson's first sport was football, not wrestling. He was such a good football player in high school that he was awarded a five-year athletic scholarship with the University of Miami. He played defensive lineman for their team, the Miami Hurricanes, from 1991 to 1995. During Johnson's years with the Hurricanes the team took the Big East Conference Championship three times and tied for the championship once.

The team's success was not due to Johnson's talents alone, though. The Miami Hurricanes have a long history of success. From the 1930s to the present, they have played in over thirty bowl games and have won more than half of them. Over the years, the Hurricanes have developed a strong connection with their fans, and fans and team members have created strong traditions. Since the 1950s, for example, games have started with the team running onto the playing field through a cloud of smoke. Accompanying the smoke is a recording of an actual hurricane. And at the beginning of the fourth quarter of every game, team and fans hold up four fingers. This means they believe that the game is won in the fourth quarter.

Troubled by injuries and depression, Johnson let his grades suffer and was suspended from the team. He was later reinstated.

see right away that it had popped from its socket. Dwayne was in tremendous pain as he was rushed to the hospital by ambulance. X-rays and MRIs confirmed a separated shoulder as well as a number of torn ligaments. The injuries required surgery and weeks of physical therapy. Dwayne was not out for a few games; he was out for the entire season.

Seriously depressed, Dwayne began skipping classes. His grades fell so low that by the end of the semester he was placed on academic probation. Although he had been a good student throughout school, his grade average had slipped to 0.7 out of a possible 4.0. This was almost as hard to take as the tackle that had knocked him out of the season.

"In that moment, I felt about as worthless as I had ever felt in my life. I had let my parents down, I had let my teammates and coaches down, and I had let myself down,"[5] he said later.

Instead of giving up and going home, though, Dwayne accepted the terms of his probation. He had to carry a paper around to all of his classes and have his professors sign it. This piece of paper was his admission slip to football practice. Without it he could not attend practice. After months of mandatory tutoring and study sessions, Dwayne had improved his grades enough to get off of probation and back on the team.

A Second Chance

Dwayne was happy to be back on the team, and he intended to keep up his grades and work hard in practice sessions to stay there. He also had another especially good experience during this time. While visiting a club with friends one evening, he met his future wife, Dany Garcia. Although she was twenty-two and nearly finished with college while he was only eighteen with several years of school ahead of him, they became a couple.

The University of Miami's football team won the Orange Bowl on January 2, 1992, and Dwayne continued to play through his next three years. But during Dwayne's senior year he suffered another injury. He ruptured two disks in his lower back. He was told to take two weeks off from football but was back on the field in just a few days. It was his senior year, and if he hoped to be

Dwayne met his wife Dany (pictured) while both were students at the University of Miami.

drafted by the NFL, he had to be seen on the field. Despite his best efforts, though, Dwayne was passed over by the NFL.

He was offered a job with the Calgary Stampeders, a Canadian team. Although he knew the pay would be very low, he needed a job. Arriving in Calgary, he learned the pay would be even lower than he originally thought. He would be only a practice player with a weekly paycheck of less than two hundred dollars. To get by, Dwayne and three other players rented a dingy apartment, which they furnished with whatever useful items they could pull from dumpsters. To eat, Dwayne went to practice sessions and meetings he did not have to attend— he knew that food would be served there.

Dwayne Johnson played in the 1992 Orange Bowl for the Miami Hurricanes. Despite success on the field he was not drafted by the NFL.

Canadian and U.S. Football: Different Countries, Different Rules

Although he had played football since he was a teenager and thought he knew all of the rules, Dwayne Johnson encountered a few surprises during his brief stint with the Canadian Football League. One thing a Canadian player might have told him is that football actually came to the United States from Canada about 130 years ago. Once in America, the size of the field changed and the rules were modified.

Actually, when written on paper, all of the differences in the rules could cover several pages. The first obvious difference is that U.S. football is played on a smaller field. This leads to one of the most basic differences; the number of players allowed on the field during the play. In Canada it is twelve players. In the United States the number is eleven. One of the most notable differences, though, is in salaries of professional football players. In Canada the salaries range from about $30,000 for rookies to $250,000 for starting quarterbacks, whereas in the United States salaries for the top NFL players can reach into the millions.

No Hope

On his lowest day, Dwayne was called into the team office. He was cut as a practice player and was being replaced by a player who had just been cut from the NFL. Dwayne was stunned. As bad as things had been, at least he had been earning a paycheck. At twenty-three, he felt like a washed-up has-been. With no hope of a position with another team in Canada or the United States, or any other job prospects, all he could think to do was fly back to Miami, to Dany.

Chapter 2

Joining the Family Business

After his experiences in Canada, Johnson's self-esteem was at an all-time low. He had returned to Miami broke, with his tail between his legs like a whipped puppy. He and Dany discussed whether or not his chances with the NFL might be any better the next year. They talked about what kind of job he might be able to find in the Miami area so he could support himself and they could remain together. They also discussed the possibility of Johnson changing careers, an idea he had been considering during part of his time in Canada. He later spoke of the time when his future was just a blank wall: "My goal was to make it in the NFL. I played with a lot of great players in college who went on to have illustrious, incredible careers and in the end it just didn't happen for me."[6]

Basically, Dany did not care what Dwayne chose to do. She would stand behind him no matter what. Dwayne knew that his parents loved him, but he could hardly believe he was lucky enough to have someone like Dany, who believed in him and loved him unconditionally. Finally, he made his decision. It would mean leaving Dany again, but at least he would not be thousands of miles away, as when he was in Canada. They would at least be able to see each other. All that remained was to phone his parents. This call was harder than the one he had made from Canada, telling them that he had been dropped from the team. He knew for certain his parents were not going to like what he was about to tell them.

Johnson credits his wife Dany (pictured) for supporting his desire to be a wrestler after being cut by the Canadian Football League.

Basic Training

Johnson knew his father would not like his decision. In fact, it would probably be easier to be slammed into the ground by a 275-pound defensive tackle (125kg) than to tell his father he wanted to become a professional wrestler. However, Johnson made the phone call. First, he asked his father to drive down from Tampa, where Johnson's parents were then living, and pick him up at Dany's apartment. Next, he told him that he wanted to become a professional wrestler, and furthermore, wanted his father to be the one to train him. Without a second's hesitation, Rocky Johnson got into his truck and made the exhausting 560-mile round trip (901.23km) to pick up his son.

The issue of his son becoming a professional wrestler, though, was another matter. He was glad to have Dwayne home with the family again, but he was not happy about his desire to become a wrestler. He was not going to give in on this matter without another kind of a fight, a verbal one. He intended to do everything he could to talk Dwayne out of what he thought was a bad decision. Rocky Johnson pulled no punches. He hit his son with every argument he had. All the way to Tampa, Johnson and his father discussed his situation. His father wanted him to be patient, wait for the next season, and give football another chance. After all, why would anyone spend four years in college just to become a wrestler and be slammed around a ring for the next thirty or so years? Then the frequent moves and financial hardships had to be considered, too.

Mapping Out His Plans

After they arrived in Tampa, many heated discussions took place during the next week as Johnson went ahead and mapped out his plans. First, he needed a job. He found one as a personal fitness trainer at a local health club. The job did not pay very well, but Johnson did not need a lot of money. What he did need was access to workout equipment, which he was free to use whenever he did not have clients or the club was not busy. Also, since the job was part-time, he had plenty of time to train to be a wrestler.

A Tough Training Schedule

Although Johnson's father was still reluctant to see his son go into the family business, if it was going to happen, then he was going to be the one to begin his son's training. From the beginning they maintained a tough training schedule. Up before daylight, father and son worked together for several hours before Johnson drove to the health club to work with his clients. When he was finished with his clients for the day, Johnson was back in the practice ring, either with his father or one of his father's friends, working on the basic moves, over and over again, until Johnson's father was satisfied that his son had the moves down just right.

Since Johnson had grown up around wrestling, he was already familiar with the vocabulary of the ring and what the names of the moves meant. When his father told him to do a certain move, he could immediately go into the correct position. For instance, one of the more common wrestling moves is called a headlock. To do a headlock, one wrestler holds his opponent's head with his arm. The body slam is a move where a wrestler picks up his opponent and slams him to the floor. Another move, and one of the most dangerous, is called the pile driver. To do this, the wrestler lifts his opponent upside down and appears to slam his opponent's head into the floor of the ring. If not done properly, this move can cause serious injury. Johnson performed every move his father called, and did them over and over. He did them as many times as his father told him to do them without complaint. Johnson understood how important it was for wrestlers to perfect every move, both to avoid injury and to put on a good show. He also wanted to perform well when it came time for his professional audition.

Training to become a wrestler was even more intense than college football training camp. As he practiced his moves, he also worked on developing what he hoped would some day become his signature moves, moves that would be identified with him. One of these moves is called the nip-up. To perform this move, the wrestler must jump straight to his feet from lying flat on the ground. He does not use his hands or even roll his body over. The move requires extreme physical agility and strength. Johnson practiced this

Under his father's tutelage, Johnson developed and practiced his signature wrestling moves and timing.

physically demanding move many times each day. He also wanted to be able to land on his feet when his opponents gave him a back-drop, which is tossing one's opponent into the air over the wrestler's back when the opponent repels off of the ropes. Johnson was not satisfied until he thought he had perfected these moves.

Pat Patterson: Friend and Mentor

Pat Patterson was one of Dwayne Johnson's earliest mentors in the ring. A friend of Rocky Johnson, Dwayne's father, and one-time opponent of Dwayne Johnson's grandfather, Peter Maivia, Patterson had a long and successful wrestling career.

Born Pierre Clemont on January 19, 1941, the Canadian wrestler chose Pat Patterson as his ring name, but altered his ring name at times. He debuted in Montreal, Quebec, in Canada in 1958 as "Pretty Boy" Pat Patterson.

To increase their popularity, many professional wrestlers adopt gimmicks. Patterson's early gimmicks included pink wrestling trunks, red lipstick, and entering the ring accompanied by a poodle. Despite his glamour gimmicks, Patterson was a "heel" during the early years of his career. A heel is a bad guy, a villain. As part of his heel persona, he wore a head mask into the ring and hid objects in the mask that made his head butts more damaging to his opponents. He turned baby-face, or good guy, in 1972 and joined the World Wrestling Federation (WWF) in 1979. In June of that year, he won the WWF North American Championship.

Retiring from the ring in 1984, Patterson became a wrestling commentator and an agent for the WWF. He was inducted into the World Wrestling Entertainment (WWE, formerly the WWF) Hall of Fame in 1996. He briefly returned to the ring in 2000, defeating Gerald Brisco with his old heel tactics. The win made him the oldest WWE Hardcore Champion. Patterson retired from the WWE in 2004.

Finally Ready

After months of grueling work, Johnson's father decided his son was ready to be evaluated by an objective professional, and so he called on his old friend, the former wrestling legend Pat Patterson. Not only was Patterson a friend of Johnson's father, he had also wrestled against his grandfather, Peter Maivia. Patterson agreed to watch Dwayne work out in the ring to see if he thought Johnson had potential as a professional wrestler. Although it was easier for Johnson to arrange such a meeting, since his family had been in the wrestling business for two generations, he knew he would not get a second chance to make a first impression. Johnson understood how important this first impression would be to his future.

Johnson had learned his basic moves. He had also worked on timing and the acting part of professional wrestling. In wrestling, acting is called "selling." In the case of a wrestling match, a good sell would be convincing the spectators that every slam against the mat is agonizing and every time the opponent has the wrestler's head in a headlock, he is about to get his neck broken. Dany was in Tampa for the weekend and attended this workout. She did not know about the selling, though, and when she saw her boyfriend being torn to pieces in the ring, or so she thought, she broke down in tears.

At the end of the session Johnson asked Patterson if he thought he was any good in the ring. Patterson's answer was very encouraging. He assured Johnson that he had the makings of a professional wrestler, and he should continue training. Johnson knew that Patterson was an honest man, and he would not make such a statement if it were not true. That was all Johnson needed to hear. If Patterson thought he had what it took to be a professional wrestler, then he would keep working toward that all-important first match.

The wait was not as long as Johnson might have expected, though. The very next week, Patterson called Johnson to tell him he was booking him on a flight to Corpus Christi, Texas, for a tryout match. Johnson was happy and excited. He called Dany in Miami and told her the news.

With his flight scheduled and the airline tickets on their way, Johnson knew he was ready for a match; however, he needed to attend to a couple of matters first. He had been wrestling in the same kinds of workout clothing a person wore to the gym. He did not own a pair of professional wrestling trunks. In order to look like a professional in the ring, he would have to be dressed properly. Second, he needed a name to use in the ring. Although they were well-known wrestlers, he did not want to use his father's or his grandfather's name. He did not want anyone to think that he had made it to the ring riding on their careers. So, since he could not think of a professional name at that time, he decided he would take his first step into the profession under his own name, Dwayne Johnson.

Dwayne Meets the WWF

In March 1996 Johnson boarded the plane for Corpus Christi and his first tryout with the World Wrestling Federation (WWF). His first professional wrestling opponent was Steve Lombardi, known as the "Brooklyn Brawler." A wrestler since the 1980s, Lombardi was one of the best-known jobbers in the business. In wrestling, a jobber is basically a professional loser. If a jobber is part of a match, it is pretty certain that his opponent will win. Johnson was excited but also nervous. After all, his future as a professional wrestler hung on this tryout. However, he had worked hard and trained well. He felt he was ready.

The match was what is known in the wrestling business as a "dark match." This means that the match was not scheduled to appear on television. Despite this, though, several important people were among the spectators. One of them was Vince McMahon, the owner of the WWF. Not surprisingly, Johnson won his first match. Even though the win was a foregone conclusion, it was Johnson's performance, the way he handled himself in the ring, that impressed McMahon and the other WWF officials present. The second half of his tryout occurred on the next night. This time his opponent was Chris Candido. Before the match, Johnson and Candido spent some time planning what they would do in the ring, almost like planning a stunt scene for a movie.

This was important if they were going to give a good show without anyone being hurt. However, this time the match went to Candido.

Johnson flew home to Tampa both anxious and encouraged. He had done a good job, given a good show, and, probably the best part of the tryout, McMahon himself had seen what the young

The Role of Vince McMahon

The chairman of the board of the WWE and a major shareholder, Vince McMahon is a wrestling promoter and film producer. In the world of professional wrestling, McMahon has been involved in a number of wrestling storylines, or angles. He also sometimes gets into the ring himself.

A second generation wrestling promoter, McMahon began his association with the wrestling business through the World Wide Wrestling Federation, a promotion started by his father Vincent J. McMahon. He promoted the first WrestleMania at Madison Square Garden in March 1985. In addition to wrestlers at this event, McMahon hired well-known pianist Liberace, the Rockettes, and pop singer Cyndi Lauper to perform. He risked most of his personal finances on the event, and it paid off. This event led to what has been called the Second Golden Age of Wrestling.

In the 1990s McMahon became heavily involved in WWF storylines as Mr. McMahon, the egotistical heel boss of the WWF, later the WWE. He was involved in feud storylines with Steve Austin, Bret Hart, and Mankind, among others. In fact, no storyline is too extreme for McMahon. In June 2007 he was supposedly blown up in a limousine. McMahon later assured CNBC that he was not actually dead. His "hands on" approach to the WWE has been instrumental in making it the only remaining major professional wrestling promotion in the United States.

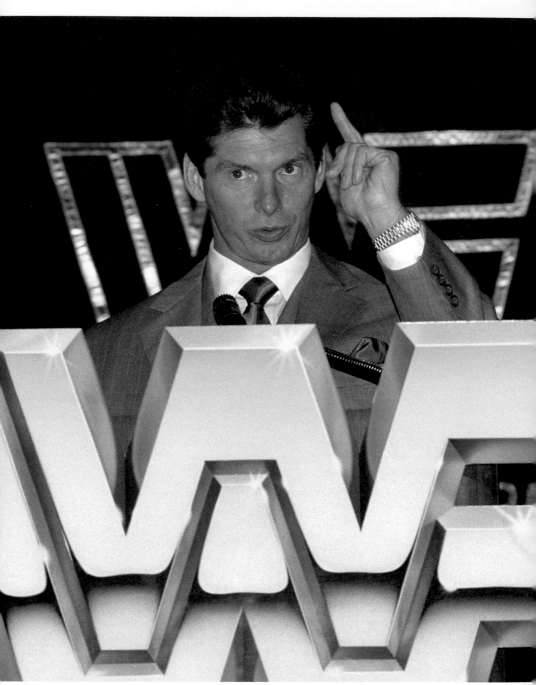

In 1996 WWF owner Vince McMahon (shown) gave Johnson an opportunity to wrestle for $150 a match.

wrestler could do in the ring. Johnson knew that if McMahon had liked the match, he would probably be back in the ring soon, this time for keeps. In the meantime, he worked, trained, and waited. The hardest part was the waiting.

First Wrestling Contract

Several days after returning to Tampa, Johnson had his answer. He received his first wrestling contract. In the beginning, his paychecks would not be much, but it was a start, and he was delighted to have the opportunity. Johnson later recalled, "It was a very basic contract. The guarantee was like $150, which was fine with me, I was happy to get that. I knew I was going to work for everything I got."[7]

First, he would go to Memphis, Tennessee, the home of the United States Wrestling Alliance (USWA). This was something like a professional football or baseball team's farm club; however, the USWA had its own stars. Though it was not a large wrestling

The USWA

The United States Wrestling Alliance was born in the Memphis, Tennessee, area in 1989. It was founded by Jeff Jarrett, Fritz Von Eric, and Jerry Lawler. They were attempting to create a third national wrestling promotion. Although it was not actually a farm club and in fact had a number of its own stars, such as Jerry "the King" Lawler, Junkyard Dog, Brian Christopher, and Dwayne Johnson, known during this time as Flex Kavana, it became a training ground for up-and-coming young wrestlers. By October 1996, though, the USWA had run its course. It disbanded after being sold to XL Sports, a group based in Cleveland, Ohio. The last USWA event, at the Big One Flea Market Pavilion, drew only 372 fans, taking in less than two thousand dollars.

promotion, or territory, the USWA was home to Jerry "the King" Lawler and Jeff Jarrett, both well-known wrestlers. Johnson knew the WWF people kept regular tabs on all of the USWA wrestlers. They received regular reports on the wrestlers and films of their matches. From the Memphis group they would choose which wrestlers would move up to the WWF.

The Long Trip

In May, just two months after his first tryout match, Johnson bought a used SUV, loaded it with his belongings, and began the 850-mile drive (1,368km) to Memphis. On the long trip Johnson had plenty of time to think about his future as a wrestler. Of course it would be hard being farther away from Dany, and making any plans for their future together had to be on hold for a while. He also needed to think of a name to use in the ring and think about what type of a character he would be. All he was sure of was that he did not want to be gimmicky, with masks and flashy costumes. As he left Tampa he did not have the answers to any of his questions. He was still determined, though, that he would not take advantage of his father's or his grandfather's name. He wanted his own ring name, something that sounded a little flashy, but also strong—a name people could remember. He settled on "Flex" for the strength part and "Kavana" as a tribute to his Samoan heritage.

Looking back on it, he realized it was not really a great name, but at the time he just needed a name, and it was the best he could do. "When I said the name aloud—Flex Kavana—it sounded like a name I could live with," Johnson said. "It had a nice marketable ring to it. One thing was for sure, nobody else had ever called themselves Flex Kavana. For better or worse, it was my name."[8]

The Dwayne Johnson who was driving to Memphis was far ahead of the young man who had flown to Canada to pursue a football career just a few months earlier. He was a more mature person. When he had flown to Canada, he had been a kid just out of college full of hopes and dreams. This trip was different. This Dwayne Johnson was a man who had experienced real-world

Johnson's first wrestling match for the USWA was a tag team match featuring Jerry Lawler, left.

disappointments and hardships. He still had hopes and dreams, but he was more realistic about what it took to turn the hopes into reality, and he also knew that sometimes dreams do not come true. However, he was willing to start at the very bottom and work his way up, whatever it took.

Paying Dues

The first news that greeted Johnson when he arrived in Memphis was a disappointment. He would not be paid $150 a match as he had first thought. As a trainee he would be paid only $40 a night. This information might have sent the old Dwayne Johnson back down the road to Tampa, but it did not faze the mature Dwayne Johnson. If he had learned one thing while in Calgary, it was how to get by on next to no money. He drove through the bleaker parts of Memphis until he found a small, cheap apartment. He signed his lease and went right to work.

In fact, only a day after arriving in Memphis, Johnson had his first wrestling event, a tag team match. As Flex Kavana, he entered the ring with a wrestler named Brian Christopher. They went against USWA star Jerry "the King" Lawler and his partner, Bill Dundee. The match became little more than a brawl, or a "schmozz" in wrestling language, but Johnson earned his first forty dollars.

Sometimes Johnson fought in professional wrestling rings, but more often than not, he fought his matches in wobbly, makeshift rings temporarily rigged on fairgrounds, asphalt parking lots, and even in barns. Other obstacles included times when the spectators were more dangerous than his opponents. Occasionally, spectators became so drunk and rowdy that they threw things at the wrestlers, causing cuts and bruises.

There were rewards, though. For example, on June 17, 1996, just a month after moving to Memphis, Johnson, as Flex Kavana, and his then–tag team partner Buzz Sawyer won the USWA Tag Team title.

His time in Tennessee also involved putting a lot of miles on his used SUV. He later described a normal Saturday's work schedule: "On Saturdays I worked a live TV show in Memphis in the morning, then drove to Nashville for a show at the Nashville Fairgrounds that evening. After that show I'd climb in my truck and drive back to Memphis. I almost never stayed overnight because I couldn't afford a hotel."[9]

On Saturdays alone, Johnson's round-trip drive was 430 miles (692km). Aside from his long drive on Saturdays, he drove to other matches outside of Memphis. All in all, Johnson put an average of 1,700 miles (2,736km) on his SUV every week. In a month's time, that added nearly 7,000 miles (11,265km) to a vehicle that was already secondhand when he bought it. Not only was he adding wear-and-tear to his vehicle, he was also spending a lot of his hard-earned money on gasoline.

Because of his low pay and the amount of money he had to spend on transportation, life in Memphis was a real challenge for the young wrestler. When it came to making ends meet, Johnson was cutting it pretty close. To make more money he sometimes sold his own autographed photographs after matches. He had kept up this exhausting pace for nearly six months when he received a call from the WWF. He was being sent to Columbus, Ohio, for another two-night tryout match.

He won the first night's match against David Haskins. Johnson's opponent the second night was the well-known wrestler Owen Hart. Hart was known for his sense of humor and his practical jokes, such as the false arm cast he wore during their match. He did not admit the cast was a fake until they were already working in the ring. Once Johnson understood he had been duped, they put on a good show. Although Hart won this match, he told McMahon that he thought Johnson was at least as good if not better than many of the wrestlers already working in the WWF. Over the years the two would become friends, but at that particular moment Johnson was basking in the praise of one of his favorite wrestlers, and it felt good.

A Lasting Bond

Johnson was a happy man when he returned to Memphis. Hart's opinion meant a lot to him. He watched videotapes of the best wrestlers in the WWF and worked harder than ever to correct

Wrestler Owen Hart, facedown on the mat, inspired Johnson to work harder and be a better wrestler.

any of his weak areas. Then, just two weeks after his match with Hart, Johnson received another phone call from the WWF. This time, they did not want him for another tryout match. He would be moving for good. He was being sent to Stamford, Connecticut, which was the headquarters of the WWF. Although he had several free days before he was expected to report to Connecticut ready to work, he immediately packed his belongings. Shortly after receiving the call, Johnson was in his SUV, pulling away from the curb. He was grateful for all that he had learned in Memphis, but he was more than ready to get started on the next step in his wrestling career. As Memphis disappeared behind him, so did the ring name Flex Kavana. Johnson was headed for Connecticut and his future with the WWF, and he still did not have a proper name for the ring.

Chapter 3

Making His Name

For a young man still in his mid-twenties, Dwayne Johnson's life had already undergone many changes. As a child, moving frequently with his family to follow his father's wrestling opportunities, he had lived in many parts of the country. He had graduated from college and gone through a very disappointing and discouraging time when his football career did not work out the way he wanted. After that, he had chosen a career that most people would find intimidating and physically demanding. Though many people enjoyed watching wrestling, very few would want to do it themselves.

For months Johnson had put in many long, hard days, paid his dues, and waited. Now, it appeared that he was going to begin enjoying the fruits of his many months of hard work. This was the most important move, the one that would really begin his wrestling career. After one more long drive, he would finally be in the big time. He would actually be a part of the World Wrestling Federation, working with the best wrestlers in the country and preparing for his WWF wrestling debut. However, the matter of a ring name was still a problem. Not only did he not have one, he could not even come up with any ideas for one. One thing at a time, though. First, he had to get to Connecticut and learn the WWF way of doing things.

One Foot in the Big Time

Johnson was put through his paces in Stamford for more than two months. He trained for many hours every day, working on different moves and routines. Even the moves he thought he knew well he learned to do better. While working to perfect his moves and routines, Johnson still needed to settle the matter of his ring name. The WWF officials suggested the name Rocky Maivia. At first Johnson resisted. He had not changed his mind about what kind of wrestler he wanted to be. He did not want costumes, body paint, or other gimmicks, and he did not want anyone to think that he had used his father's and his grandfather's careers to get him into the WWF. However, the officials convinced him that by using parts of his father's and grandfather's names, he was not trading on their careers; he was honoring them. Once it was explained to him that way, and after discussing it with Dany and his family, Johnson decided he could use the name with a clear conscience. After all, he had a great deal of respect for both his father and his late grandfather.

Madison Square Garden

Madison Square Garden is probably one of the most famous sports and entertainment arenas in the United States. Called the Garden by local New Yorkers, the current Madison Square Garden, the fourth by the same name, was built in 1968 above a working railroad line. The name Madison Square Garden has two sources. One is the location of the first Garden, at 26th Street and Madison Avenue. The other is Madison Square Park, a beautiful nineteenth-century garden and park located in New York City.

The current Garden underwent a $200 million renovation in 1991. Today, it is the home of the New York Rangers hockey team, the New York Knicks basketball team, and the New York Liberty ladies' basketball team. It is also a home arena of the WWE, the site of several WrestleMania and SummerSlam events. In addition to sports, the Garden also hosts many popular music events and graduation ceremonies. It is also the site where the Ringling Bros. and Barnum & Bailey Circus is staged when it comes to New York City.

Before a packed house, Johnson debuts in 1996 in the Survivor Series in Madison Square Garden in New York City.

Finally, on November 17, 1996, the newly named Rocky Maivia made his official WWF debut in the WWF Survivor Series in Madison Square Garden in New York City. This was by far the most important day in Dwayne Johnson's life. The Garden was far different from any other place he had wrestled. He was awed by the sheer size of the place. Johnson had been used to much smaller crowds. The matches he fought in makeshift rings on parking lots drew dozens to maybe as much as a couple of hundred wrestling fans. The smaller arenas held several hundred. Madison Square Garden had seating for up to twenty thousand wrestling fans.

In addition to being a huge facility, the Garden was careful about security. No behavior problems with unruly fans were tolerated at Madison Square Garden. Rules concerning fan conduct were in writing. Fans were to be respectful to those around them. They could not interfere with the events in any way. Offensive language, fighting, and throwing objects were not tolerated. Whether or not they drank alcohol, the fans were responsible for their own behavior. This meant that all the wrestlers had to worry about were their opponents, not the behavior of the spectators. In the event some fans chose to test the rules, security personnel were on hand to enforce them.

The Garden has an impressive history. The current Garden, opened in 1968, four years before Johnson was born, was actually the fourth Madison Square Garden. The first one opened in 1879. Since its creation, the Garden has had the reputation of hosting world-class sporting events and the best of entertainment. When Dwayne Johnson, aka Rocky Maivia, stepped into the ring at Madison Square Garden that November day, he was not just performing in his first WWF event, he was becoming part of the history of the Garden.

A Learning Process

For this match, eight wrestlers, four to a team, would fight until all of the members of one team had been pinned. Rocky Maivia was teamed with Jake Roberts, Marc Mero, and Barry Windham. Their opponents were Jerry Lawler, Crush, Goldust, and WWF

Intercontinental Champion Hunter Hearst Helmsley. In addition to the huge crowd in the Garden, the event was also televised via pay-per-view. The spectators in the crowd and the viewers at home had one thing in common: Few if any of them had heard of Dwayne Johnson, and no one had ever heard of Rocky Maivia. Since his new persona was unknown, when Rocky Maivia entered the WWF ring that first time, the fan response was lukewarm, at best.

First, Roberts took down Lawler, then Goldust pinned Windham. This left three men standing on each team. When Mero pinned Helmsley and Crush pinned Roberts, each team was down to two men. Maivia was one of the two remaining members still on his feet. First, Maivia pinned Crush, then he took down Goldust. Half an hour after entering the ring, Rocky Maivia had pinned his team's last opponent to the mat, and his team had won the match. It had been an impressive debut for Rocky Maivia, and Johnson knew that every wrestling fan, at home or in the Garden, who had seen the match would remember his new ring name. This win began the process of building his reputation as a professional wrestler. Johnson knew he was still very much in a learning process, though, and his matches were pretty much warm-ups for the headlining bouts. At this point in his career, he basically smiled at the fans and kept his mouth shut. He was concentrating on his performance as a wrestler, not on developing a personality to support his ring name.

First Success

Rocky Maivia's first major success occurred just a few months after that first match in Madison Square Garden. On February 13, 1997, with just three months of experience as a WWF wrestler, he won the Intercontinental Championship by defeating Paul Michael Levesque, known as Triple H. This win made Johnson the youngest Intercontinental Champion in the history of the WWF. He was three months short of his twenty-fifth birthday. Johnson was happy with the direction his career was moving. He was appearing in many matches throughout the country, winning an impressive number of these matches and starting to become

Because Johnson was attractive and young looking, he was labeled a baby-face—a good-guy wrestler with a clean image.

a "name" as a professional wrestler. However, when it came to his ring character, the polite, smiling Rocky Maivia, something was missing. At the time, Johnson thought the problem was that he had taken this title so early in his career that the fans simply were not buying it, as though they thought the championship had come to him too easily. But then the fans had no way of knowing about all of the work he had done to get ready for his first championship match. Even though the "win" had already been scripted, professional matches have to be well rehearsed and the wrestlers have to be in top physical form so they will not be injured. Whatever the reason, though, baby-face Rocky Maivia was not getting the kind of fan response Dwayne Johnson wanted for him.

Baby-face Blues

Johnson was a very attractive young man with a dazzling smile and a pleasant personality. These were the same qualities he brought into the ring as Rocky Maivia. Because of this, he was labeled a baby-face, or face. In wrestling terms, a baby-face is a good guy, a wrestler with a clean image who is usually on the fans' good side. In fact, fans usually cheer for the good guys but not in Rocky Maivia's case. Not only did the fans not cheer him, they actually jeered him and threw verbal insults as he walked down the aisle and entered the ring for his matches.

Despite the mostly unexpected fan reaction, though, Johnson stayed with the role of baby-face throughout the rest of his first season with the WWF, ignoring the taunts and smiling as he approached wrestling rings in the United States, Europe, and the Middle East. He also kept his head down and mostly stayed to himself during the long traveling time. No one on the tours knew him very well, and he really did not know any of them. One exception was Bret Hart, who, like his brother Owen, befriended the twenty-four-year-old wrestler, a kindness Johnson never forgot.

However, Johnson was making his name, and his income had improved dramatically. For that alone, he could handle a few insults and some lonely days. He did, however, draw some favorable attention. During his first short season with the WWF, he was number three among the candidates for Rookie of the Year.

Johnson stayed with the role of a baby-face throughout his first season with the WWF.

Learning the Angles

As he wrestled in different parts of the country, Johnson became involved in angles, which are carefully staged and planned fictional storylines played out in the ring. Some angles involve single matches; others, however, are played out over several years. Angles are played as long as the storyline and the wrestlers in-

Two wrestlers play out one of their angles—carefully planned and staged fictional storylines played out in the ring.

volved are popular with the fans. The success of the angle is based on the strength of fan response.

As Johnson knew when he entered the business, although wrestlers are highly trained athletes engaging in a potentially dangerous sport, wrestling is still entertainment— acting, with a lot of very physical stage prowess. As in other forms of entertainment it is all about the show and showmanship, selling the angle. Just like actors in stage plays, wrestlers follow cues. These cues let the wrestlers know what is supposed to happen next during the match. By following the cues, wrestlers can make their battles in the ring look real and sell the match to the fans. The cues also lessen the possibility of being injured. Like a play in rehearsal, wrestlers will work before a match to plan their spots, moves designed to get a certain type of reaction from the fans. Sometimes a spot does not work as planned. This is called a blown spot. A highspot can be either a top-rope move or a series of moves that appear to be particularly dangerous and usually draw a "pop," or a big response, from the fans.

A no-show can also be part of an angle. A no-show is a wrestler not showing up for a match. No-shows are usually staged as part of a storyline. Very seldom do wrestlers simply not show up for matches because this can result in being fined or fired.

Johnson, however, followed the rules and played by the numbers. He was a good guy both inside and outside of the ring. WWF officials told him to keep smiling and acting like he was glad to be there. So, no matter how hard it was to keep smiling while half of the fans in the arenas were hurling insults, that was exactly what he did—for as long as he could.

In the spring of 1997 Johnson's parents and his girlfriend Dany came to Chicago to watch him in a match. Rocky Maivia was defending his Intercontinental title against a heel character called the Sultan. Rocky Maivia successfully defended his title, beating the Sultan and the match even got a good "pop," or favorable crowd reaction, from the spectators. Despite this, though, the jeers and insults continued as he left the ring. Neither Johnson, his family, nor Dany could understand the crowd's reaction. The spectators shouted "Die Rocky, Die" and worse. Not content to just shout insults, the fans even began making insulting signs and holding them up during the matches.

However, Johnson reached the point where he could no longer ignore the jeering and insults. He continued to do his job in the ring, and do it well, but he stopped smiling. Finally, something happened that gave Johnson the opportunity to take some downtime and to change Rocky Maivia's personality for good.

Downtime and Major Changes

Later in the spring of 1997 two important events occurred. First, Owen Hart won Rocky Maivia's International title. Second, in a match with Mankind, Johnson suffered a knee injury that forced him to take some time away from the wrestling business. To recover properly, Johnson would have to stay out of the ring for at least two months. Johnson put this time to good use. He and Dany had already become engaged, and so they planned to have their wedding during his recovery time. By now Johnson had earned a name in the wrestling business, but Dany's parents were not particularly impressed. Although he was successful, he was still a wrestler. They knew wrestlers spent a lot of time on the road and that an injury could end his career. Because of this and other issues, they were very resistant to the idea of their daughter marrying him. However, they knew the couple was determined to be married, and so they put aside their personal differences to help the pair plan a unique wedding celebration, a family event that would honor Dany's Cuban background as well as Johnson's Samoan culture.

Dany and Dwayne Johnson were married in an outdoor ceremony on May 3, 1997, the day after Johnson's twenty-fifth birthday. The bride wore a beautiful traditional white gown with a flowing train and carried a cascading bouquet. The groom was classically handsome in a black tuxedo. With his best man Uliuli Fifita, the wrestler known as Haku, standing by, the couple said their vows beneath an arch of flowers.

After the ceremony wedding guests were entertained by a Polynesian band and dancers. Johnson's mother even performed a traditional Samoan wedding dance, and the wedding banquet was similar to a Hawaiian luau. In another departure from traditional receptions, in addition to a wedding cake the guests were served chocolate chip cookies, one of the groom's favorite treats. The number of guests was larger than the couple first expected. In fact, as a sign of respect, many of Johnson's Samoan relatives traveled great distances to witness his marriage and take part in the celebration. Dany's and Johnson's parents finally met for the first time at the wedding. This could have been a tense time, but everyone put aside their personal opinions to support Johnson and his new bride on their day. If the ice was not completely broken between Johnson and Dany's family, it had at least begun to thaw.

Johnson was happy to have Dany as his wife, and even though it was a happy moment in his life and one he had wanted for a long time, marriage was still a major change for him. However, this was not the only way his life was changing at this time. Johnson was preparing to make a big change in his career as well. This change would require completely overhauling the personality of Rocky Maivia, because Johnson did not want to go back to work as a baby-face. Fortunately, the WWF officials were in total agreement with him about making the change from baby-face to heel. In fact, once he was recovered from his injury and ready to go back to work, they asked him to join the Nation of Domination. The Nation, as it was called, was a "stable," or group of wrestlers who share some common element. The Nation was composed of a group of "heels," or bad-guy characters, and was led by Ron Simmons, known in the ring as Faarooq. Other members of the Nation at that time were D'Lo Brown and Kama Mustafa.

Ron Simmons: The Rock's Rival

The name Ron Simmons may mean little to wrestling fans, but the name Faarooq is sure to ring a bell. In the 1990s, Faarooq was the leader of the Nation of Domination, a stable, or group, of mostly African American wrestlers. His leadership of the Nation, as the group was called, ended in 1998 at the hands of the Rock.

Though professional rivals, Faarooq and the Rock had similar backgrounds. Simmons was born in 1958 in Marietta, Georgia, but like the Rock, his first sport was football. Simmons was a high school football star and then attended Florida State University. From 1977 to 1980, with Simmons playing defensive nose guard, the Florida State University football team, the Seminoles, was nearly unstoppable. The team played in Orange Bowl championships during Simmons's junior and senior years. While still at Florida State, Simmons was inducted into the Orange Bowl Hall of Fame. After university, Simmons spent the first half of the 1980s playing professional football, first with the Cleveland Browns, and then with the Tampa Bay Bandits.

In 1986 Simmons was recruited into wrestling by Japanese wrestler Hiro Matsuda, who also trained him. Simmons made his professional wrestling debut in the fall of that year. His full-time wrestling career spanned more than twenty years. He is currently involved in public relations work with the WWE.

The Heel

Johnson's first appearance as a heel took place in Jackson, Mississippi, in August of 1997. After an absence of more than two months, Rocky Maivia rocked wrestling fans when he made his official debut as a bad guy. Faarooq was pinned by the wrestler Chainz. Maivia jumped into the ring on a "run in." A run in is a wrestler who is not actively participating in a match jumping into the ring to come to the aid of one of the wrestlers.

The fans expected Maivia to play his usual baby-face role by helping Chainz, who was also a good guy. They were shocked when he came to Faarooq's aid instead and choke-slammed Chainz. Although he was already committed to them privately, this was Rocky Maivia's very public uniting with the Nation. Rocky Maivia was thoroughly and loudly booed by the fans. The noise level was incredible. He had been booed and jeered before, but this was different. The fans were showing enthusiasm for Rocky Maivia like they had never shown it before.

Johnson had been waiting for this very kind of fan response for his ring character for a long time. In the wrestling business, this is called a push, something that causes a wrestler to gain in popularity. In this case, Rocky Maivia had become a wrestler the fans loved to hate.

However, Johnson had one concern about being part of the Nation. At this time, the Nation of Domination was composed almost entirely of African American wrestlers. At first Johnson was worried that joining the Nation would make him appear to be a racist, aligned only with people of his race, and having been on the receiving end of racism at different times in his own life, that was the last thing he wanted wrestling fans to think of him. Young people watched the matches and, even though he had turned heel, Rocky Maivia was still a role model. He intended to set the record straight immediately. He wanted his fans to know exactly why he had chosen to join the Nation and that it had nothing to do with the color of anyone's skin. He said, "Joining the Nation wasn't a black thing. It wasn't a white thing. It was a respect thing. And one way or another, from now on, Rocky Maivia is going to get some respect . . . by any means necessary."[10]

The Nation of Domination

The Nation of Domination was a militant "heel" stable in the WWF for two years, from November 1996 to November 1998. Loosely based on the Nation of Islam, the group was originally led by Faarooq. Members of the Nation during its lifetime included J.C. Ice, Wolfie D, Crush, D'Lo Brown, Savio Vega, Kama Mustafa, and Ahmed Johnson.

The beginning of the end for the Nation occurred due to an emerging feud between Faarooq and the Rock, who had turned heel and joined the Nation. Ultimately, the Rock succeeded in defeating Faarooq and putting him out. The personality of the Nation then changed from militant to cool and gimmicky. The Rock's popularity incited jealousy among other members of the Nation, who finally jumped the Rock. This assault ultimately led to the disbanding of the Nation.

As a bad guy, this reborn version of Rocky Maivia had a lot to say. In fact, he was so outspoken it was sometimes hard to shut him up. When his fans booed and jeered at him during matches, he jeered right back at them, often grabbing the microphone from the announcer and hurling insults of his own from the ring. Sometimes he called them a bunch of jabronis—slang for "nobodies." He even insulted fans during prerecorded promotion spots. Surprisingly, the fans loved it. They went for the new Rocky Maivia in a big way.

Chapter 4

Introducing the Rock

From his brief season of Canadian football to shortly after his marriage to Dany in May 1997, Dwayne Johnson had gone from a jobless college graduate with less than ten dollars in his pocket to a headlining professional wrestler. The success had not come easily, though. He had stayed in slum apartments and lived on the cheapest food he could buy or did without. He had also endured long, grueling days of training for many months and suffered his share of sprains, bumps, and bruises as he learned his craft. Finally, his training and other travel had taken him away from Dany for long periods of time. Now, though, the time was at hand when Johnson could enjoy the benefits of the sacrifices he had made. His new era began with a name.

The Rock Is in the House

Changing from Rocky Maivia to the Rock came about as part of a storyline, an angle. With each new match, Rocky Maivia gained in confidence and also in brashness. He went from being a smiling, polite, mild-mannered baby-face to a brash, cocky, arrogant, in-your-face heel, and it was working very well for him. The fans were responding to this rude, arrogant character with a great deal of enthusiasm.

According to the angle, Maivia was involved in a long-standing feud with the equally brash and mouthy Stone Cold Steve Austin. The feud was all for the public, though; privately Johnson and

Johnson and Stone Cold Steve Austin (right) played out a public feud as part of a promotion for their championship bout. Austin won the match but Johnson won the fans.

Austin got along very well. In fact, Austin made statements to the effect that he and Johnson actually brought out the best in each other in the ring.

According to the angle, the two were taking their feud into the ring, a challenge for Austin's Intercontinental Championship belt. Rocky Maivia's public challenge made WWF wrestling history. It changed his name. "Stone Cold Steve Austin, I'm challenging you for the Intercontinental championship," Johnson taunted, "and if you have any manhood at all, you'll accept my challenge. And if you do accept my challenge, then your bottom line will say: 'Stone Cold—has-been. Compliments of . . . The Rock!'"[11]

A Public Feud

This statement started a wildfire of words and insults between the Rock and Austin which increased in intensity in the weeks leading up to the match. This was good for Johnson because interest in the Rock also ramped up considerably as the well-publicized feud with Austin progressed toward the big grudge match, the challenge for Austin's championship belt. By the time of the actual match, in December 1997, Johnson's alter ego had pretty much achieved superstar status and the Rock had become a household name among wrestling fans. The match, a pay-per-view event, was held on December 7 in Springfield, Massachusetts. Whatever the fans were expecting when they crowded into the stadium for the event, it certainly was not what they witnessed. Since Austin was a heel, too, he fought dirty and won the match. He did this by driving his truck to the ring as though he were trying to run down someone, and, among other things, put one of his signature moves, a stunner, on a referee. He also used the move to bring down the Rock.

Austin had the belt, but, according to the angle, McMahon, the owner of the WWF, was furious at the outcome. He said that Austin had used his truck as a weapon and ordered a rematch the next night. Rather than turning over the belt, though, Austin put the stunner on McMahon, and also according to the storyline, threw the championship belt into a nearby river. McMahon awarded the championship to the Rock as a forfeit. Many fans did not like the way the Rock got the belt, and it brought him more attention. As the Rock, Johnson said later in an interview:

> Hey, is it my fault that Austin was afraid to get into the ring with me again? . . . He gave up the title to me rather than lose it in the ring, which is exactly what would have happened. He knew it, I knew it, everybody knew it. Austin's a coward. He'll come out there with his big truck, or he'll attack the Rock from behind, but when it came to a face-to-face match, he wanted no part of that. Where's his guts?[12]

Regardless of how he obtained the championship belt, though, the win meant more publicity for the Rock, and as anyone in the wrestling business knows, any publicity is good publicity. Despite his brash character, though, the Rock had a code of behavior. If an opponent beat him fairly, the Rock would admit it publicly, with a few appropriate "wait until next time" statements thrown in so no one would think the Rock was getting soft. Winning or losing, however, was not the issue. It was all about the publicity and the ratings—whatever brought in the fans. And the fans were showing up in droves to see what this big-mouth character called the Rock was going to do next. Whatever it was, it was sure to be entertaining. The more fans, the more tickets and pay-per-view fees. The more tickets and pay-per-view, the more money for the WWF. It was the sort of situation in which everybody in the business won, and one of the biggest winners was the Rock.

Talking Trash and Mega Moves

Over time the Rock became, if anything, even more brash and arrogant. Most people refer to themselves in the first person. The Rock, however, referred to himself in the third person. For instance, if he made a statement about an upcoming match, he would not say, "I will win this match." He would say, "The Rock will win." However, he would phrase it much more colorfully. In fact, some of the Rock's quotes became part of the wrestling scene. He once said, "The Rock will take you down Know Your Role Boulevard, which is on the corner of Jabroni Drive and check you straight into the Smackdown Hotel!"[13]

The Rock persona developed by Johnson had a reputation for being brash and bold but fair.

When making announcements in the ring or giving interviews, the Rock could not bring himself to say something as commonplace as "Do you understand?" Instead he would say "Do you smell what The Rock is cooking?" He was big, arrogant, and very vocal. In fact, many said the Rock had a big mouth, yet he also had the size and skill to back up whatever he said.

He fed on the jeers and taunts of wrestling fans. He was getting exactly what he wanted, becoming one of the best-known heels in the business. For the Rock, any attention was good attention. The fans even reacted wildly when he raised his right eyebrow. He called this the "People's Eyebrow."

Meanwhile, in another angle, jealousy was brewing among the Nation over the attention the Rock was getting. In fact, Faarooq, the leader of the Nation, did not like it at all. After all, he, Faarooq, not the Rock, was the leader of the Nation. The Rock was only the new guy on the team. Jealousy continued to mount. With two such strong personalities, it was not long before a full-blown power struggle for leadership of the Nation began.

The Feud Builds

As usual, the Rock, always the attention-grabber, had something arrogant to say:

> I've got power because I've got the belt. What's he [Faarooq] got? He has a big mouth, but he doesn't have anything else going for him. The Rock is the leader of this group. The Rock is the best Intercontinental champ in history. I've proven myself. The Nation of Domination is mine. The Rock is just better suited to being a leader. If Faarooq really thought about things, he'd realize he's better off taking a lesser role with The Nation.[14]

The feud with Faarooq came to a head during a match between the Rock and Ken Shamrock during WrestleMania XIV on March 29, 1998. Although both wrestlers were heels, the Rock had gone by the rules during the match; Shamrock did not. Shamrock chose to ignore the referees and refused to break a hold on the Rock when the referees ordered him to stop. When they tried to physically break his hold, Shamrock slammed all of the referees to the mat and pinned the Rock, who appeared to have incurred a leg injury. Although Faarooq was ringside, he did nothing to help his teammate who was suffering under Shamrock. Despite his illegal moves, Shamrock thought he had won the match. However, due to his behavior in the ring, the decision was reversed. The Rock retained his Intercontinental title.

Although he still had his title, the Rock was angry because Faarooq had not helped him in the ring when Shamrock had been trying to break his leg. The other members of the Nation were

Drugs and Other Health Issues

Although the outcomes of most professional wrestling matches are determined in advance, wrestling can still be hard on the health of the performers. Many professional wrestlers are on the road three hundred or more days out of the year. If they have downtime due to accidents, they lose money, so some wrestlers work despite painful injuries. Some turn to painkillers. Although painkillers numb the pain, they also make the wrestlers feel tired and slow. Because of this, they take other drugs to speed up their bodies so they can perform. Not only is this mixture of drugs dangerous in the short term, it is also addictive.

Another drug problem that the wrestling industry as well as other professional sports contends with is steroid use. Wrestlers have to have big, strong bodies. They can make their bodies large by gaining a large amount of weight, which can be a danger to their health. Instead, some turn to steroids to bulk up. However, steroid abuse can also affect the minds of its users. They sometimes become violent and out of control, as in the case of Chris Benoit, who allegedly killed his wife and child and then took his own life on June 25, 2007.

angry, as well. They felt Faarooq had betrayed the Nation by not coming to the aid of a teammate. Because of his bad behavior, the team kicked Faarooq out of the Nation. Of course, this began another major feud, leaving the Rock and Faarooq bitter enemies. The new feud brought larger crowds to their supposed grudge matches. One of these matches was the "Unforgiven" pay-per-view event in April 1998, when Faarooq, Shamrock, and Steve Blackman defeated Faarooq's former teammates, the Rock, Brown, and Mark Henry. Of course, what these well-publicized events actually did was made a lot of money for the WWF and increased

the popularity of the wrestlers as well as their income. In the fall of 1998, Johnson signed a new contract with the WWF that would earn him a minimum of $400,000 a year. In addition to his new contract, the Rock made another career change. He left the Nation and joined another group, the Corporation, which had been formed by Vince and Shane MacMahon in the fall of 1998. Among the Corporation were the Big Bossman, Commissioner of Slaughter, also called Sergeant Slaughter, Pat Patterson, and Gerald Brisco. The Rock was billed as the Crown Jewel of the Corporation.

He now referred to himself as "the People's Champion." He had a signature move called the "People's Elbow" which he used to "lay the smack down," defeating his opponents. Of course, the name, the character, and the words were all a part of the whole entertainment package. Whether the Rock was winning against Mankind and Ken Shamrock in Breakdown— The Steel Cage Match or losing the Intercontinental title to Triple H, both of which occurred in 1998, the Rock was still a winner because each match increased his popularity. As the Rock's popularity rose, Dwayne Johnson's income rose, whether from WWF contracts, endorsements, or other opportunities. This all meant money in the bank and financial security for Dwayne and Dany Johnson.

By 1998 Johnson's status as the Rock had made him a celebrity. He appeared on television as "the People's Champion."

Different Sides of Fame

By now Johnson and Dany were living in a home with closets that were probably larger than some of the ratty apartments Johnson had occupied in Calgary and Memphis. The secondhand SUV was long gone. They no longer needed to be on a tight budget and could pretty much afford whatever they wanted in the way of homes, entertainment, food, clothing, and vacations. This was because not only was Johnson successful as a wrestler, Dany was also a successful businesswoman, a financial planner.

The couple had everything money could buy, but the fame and fortune came at a high price. For instance, Johnson and his wife lost much of their privacy. They could no longer take a walk in the neighborhood, go shopping at the mall, or go out to a movie without being mobbed by fans. While many fans were polite and waited for an appropriate moment to approach Johnson to have their picture taken with the Rock, others were rude, pushy, and demanding. In fact, sometimes they would physically push Dany out of their way, shoving themselves between her and her husband. Whatever the behavior of the fans, though, outside the ring Johnson was unfailingly courteous, thoughtful, and polite, especially with his youngest fans, the children. He knew that many of them looked up to the Rock and wanted to be like him. Because of this, one way Johnson put his fame to good use was by always trying to be a good role model. He once said,

> There's a huge responsibility. It's extremely important to me, outside of the ring, outside of the character, that these kids realize you have to go to school, get your grades, make sure your grades are up, and do the right thing. It's hard in this day and age to escape the peer pressure. But, believe me, look peer pressure in the face and tell those other guys who want you to do drugs or to take pills or take crack or smoke whatever it is, and say, "Hey, I'm going to do the right thing." It's just that simple.[15]

Johnson knew that fame had other downsides as well, such as getting a swelled head and becoming too impressed with one's reputation. Sometimes, whether in wrestling or any other enter-

Before Their Time

Owen Hart's 1999 death resulting from a mishap during a stunt at Kemper Arena in Kansas City occurred before thousands of wrestling fans. Hart was not the only wrestler to die young but most wrestlers died outside the ring. A few, like Frank "Bruiser Brody" Goodish and Dino Bravo, died violently. Goodish was stabbed to death during a fistfight in Puerto Rico in 1988. Bravo was gunned down, gangland style, in his Quebec apartment in 1993.

Other wrestlers died as a result of drug and alcohol abuse. This list includes Louie Spicoli, lady wrestler Miss Elizabeth, and Crash Holly.

A surprising number of wrestlers have died as the result of heart attacks. This includes Eddie Guerrero, who succumbed to heart failure in his Minneapolis hotel room in 2005 at the age of thirty-five. Other heart-related deaths include Road Warrior Hawk, dead from a heart attack at forty-two; Hercules Hernandez, who suffered a fatal heart attack at forty-seven; Big Bossman, heart failure at forty-two; and the British Bulldog, Davey Boy Smith, dead from a heart attack at thirty-nine. Experts attribute some of these deaths to long-term steroid use and some to the repeated blunt-force trauma of wrestling matches, while others are due to natural causes, such as family history of heart disease.

tainment field, when people become stars they lose sight of who put them there, and the people who put them there are the fans. Johnson knew firsthand that some big names in the entertainment industry refused to talk to fans, give autographs, or have their pictures taken.

He had also seen colleagues in the wrestling business abuse and misuse the opportunities fame had brought them. Some were involved in public brawls and other out-of-control behavior. Some damaged their minds and bodies with drugs. Alcohol and drug abuse had even taken the lives of wrestlers and other sports figures. Johnson chose not to go down that path. He respected his life, his family, his health, and all of the opportunities he had been given. He would not waste them.

Another wise move Johnson made was keeping his eyes open for any of the variety of opportunities that came his way. By now, wrestlers, like other sports figures, were earning additional income from product endorsements and appearing on television programs other than sporting events. Sometimes they had cameo roles in television comedies and dramas. Cameos are brief roles with few spoken lines. For some, these cameo roles led to larger parts, both on television and in the movies. Johnson carefully considered each opportunity he was offered, and when a good one came along he took advantage of it. However, it was wrestling that had made him rich and famous. For a while longer, it remained his main focus.

Tragedy

Johnson was not about to drop his wrestling career and jump into an acting career, something he knew little about, but he did consider his options as he continued wrestling. Johnson appreciated all of the benefits that came along with the increased popularity of professional wrestling and especially the popularity of his character, the Rock. He had earned his success, though, as well as the friendship of some of his former wrestling idols.

The last months of the 1990s and the first years of the twenty-first century brought both triumph and tragedy into Johnson's personal and professional life. One of the saddest events in his life occurred on May 23, 1999, in Kansas City, Missouri. The Rock and the other wrestlers were in their dressing rooms, waiting to be called to the ring for their own matches. In the meantime, Johnson's friend and former mentor, Owen Hart, waited high above the crowd in the arena's rafters, ready to perform one of his scene-stealing stunts. According to the plan, he would be lowered from the arena's ceiling and into the ring by a cable to make a grand entrance for his match, a stunt he had performed previously. Some say the cable snapped. Others say he became disconnected from it. Whatever the cause, Hart plunged over 50 feet

Emergency medical workers try to revive Owen Hart, who died in a ring accident in 1999 while Johnson was backstage.

(15m) to his death. Fans and performers alike were stunned and heartbroken by the accident. Owen Hart, the incorrigible jokester, had been a beloved member of the wrestling community. One teenage onlooker said, "We thought it was a doll at first. We thought they were just playing with us. We were really shocked when we found out that it was no joke."[16]

Having to go into the ring such a short time after Hart was taken away by ambulance was one of the hardest things the Rock and the other wrestlers had ever had to do in their wrestling careers, but they did it. In the entertainment industry, the show must go on. While wrestling is a sport, it is also entertainment, so, putting aside their personal feelings, the wrestlers took their turns in the ring. However, all storylines and scripts planned for

From WWF to WWE

The World Wrestling Federation announced its name change to World Wrestling Entertainment, Inc., on May 6, 2002. One issue causing the name change was the World Wildlife Fund, which also used the WWF logo. Another reason for the change had to do with the growing diversity of entertainment properties connected with the organization.

Linda McMahon, CEO of WWE and wife of Vince McMahon explained the change: "As World Wrestling Federation Entertainment, we have entertained millions of fans around the United States and around the globe. Our new name puts the emphasis on the "E" for entertainment, what our company does best. WWE provides us with a global identity that is distinct and unencumbered, which is critical to our U.S. and international growth plans."

WWE is headquartered in Stamford, Connecticut, and has offices in New York City, Chicago, London, England, and Toronto, Canada.

World Wide Entertainment, Inc., news release, May 6, 2002. www.corporate.wwe.com/news/2002/2002/_05_06.jsp.

the following night's event were scrapped, and the program was dedicated as a tribute to Owen Hart.

Big Changes

Johnson had his share of wins as well as losses the last six months of 1999. He beat Billy Gunn in the SummerSlam in August, and with Mick Foley, won the Tag Team titles from the Undertaker and the Big Show in September. And again with Foley, he won the Armageddon match against the New Age Outlaws on December 12.

However, in addition to wrestling, Johnson had the chance to try several other things. He was involved in writing his autobiography, released in 1999, titled *The Rock Says . . . .* This book ultimately reached number one on the *New York Times* best seller list. He also made his acting debut, both on television and in the movies. He had several television roles including one episode of *That Seventies Show*, titled "That Wrestling Show," in which he played his father, Rocky Johnson, and one episode of *The Net*, in which he played the character Brody. In March 2000 he guest hosted *Saturday Night Live*, acting in several skits, and he played the Champion in an episode of *Star Trek: Voyager*. He also had a cameo role as a mugger in the motion picture *The Long Shot*, filmed in 2000.

Johnson's first big movie role, though, was as Mathayus the Scorpion King in *The Mummy Returns*, which was released in 2001. In order to act in this film, he had to take some time off from his WWF duties. Although he was very happy to have a significant role in a major motion picture, 2001 was a special year for another reason. His wife Dany gave birth to their daughter, 7-pound, 10-ounce Simone Alexandra (3.5kg), born August 14 in Davie, Florida. Next to his wedding day, the birth of his daughter was the most important milestone in Johnson's life. Despite the Rock's tough guy image, with his little daughter Johnson was a total softie. In a recent interview the wrestler and action movie star openly admitted he is totally in his daughter's control: "I'm wrapped around both of her little fingers! I'll do anything to keep that smile on her face."[17]

Johnson took time off from wrestling to do his first movie role as the Scorpion King in the film **The Mummy Returns.**

Johnson is a hands-on parent. His devotion to his daughter and his ability to step away from any tough guy or celebrity persona and proudly and openly admit the power his daughter has over him only adds to his approval ratings. His popularity has led to a number of games and promotional items. The Rock and some of the movie characters Johnson has portrayed have appeared in a number of computer games and as action figures. Even after acting for several years, Johnson still gets a kick out of seeing these characters leaping across the computer screen or in toy stores. Despite his success Johnson takes none of this for granted: "It never gets old for me, whether it's seeing myself in a video game or as an action figure or on a movie poster or in a movie trailer—it never gets old or lost on me."[18]

Chapter 5

Knowing Your Roles

"**K**now your role" was one of the Rock's most famous catch-phrases. In the wrestling business, this meant the other wrestler should know his place, be himself, and not get out of line. In the Rock's brash way, this statement was something of a put-down for his opponents in the ring. As Dwayne Johnson made the transition into acting, though, "Know your role" took on several different meanings. In fact, Johnson is involved in a number of different kinds of roles. In acting, Johnson has to know his character and his lines. Additionally, his roles as an actor and a celebrity, as well as being a full-time father, will keep him a busy man for many years to come.

Television and Movies Beckon

With being a star of the wrestling world, writing a best-selling autobiography, and appearing in movies and on television, Johnson had been maintaining a grueling schedule. Between wrestling commitments and movie offers, he worked long days and had to spend a great deal of time away from his home and his family. This was the most difficult part of being an in-demand celebrity. The long separations were hard for Johnson and his family.

More movie roles awaited him, and he was invited to host *Saturday Night Live* a second time, but he also had the remainder of his WWF contract to honor. As busy as his schedule was, though, he managed to make it work and honored his many obligations.

In the 2002 movie The Scorpion King *Johnson had his first starring role.*

For instance, in February 2001 he beat Kurt Angle to win the WWF title and defeated Booker T at the SummerSlam in July 2001 to win the WCW title. He won the Tag Team title with Chris Jericho at RAW in October of that year and took back the WCW title he lost to Jericho in early November. However, in December 2001 he once again lost the WCW title to Jericho.

With the direction his life was taking, Johnson had already begun to trim down his wrestling schedule. He began to cut back even more in 2002. As Johnson began to phase out his life as a wrestler, the WWF was going through some changes of its own. On May 2, 2002, the WWF officially changed its name to World Wrestling Entertainment, or WWE. During this year, the Rock had some memorable matches with Jericho, the Undertaker, and Hulk Hogan, whom he beat at WrestleMania X8 in March of that year.

Johnson's second appearance on *Saturday Night Live* took place the following month. Comedian and actor Ray Romano had originally been scheduled to host the segment but had to back out. Johnson was called on to host a second time, and the event made *SNL* history. Johnson became the first athlete to host the show a second time.

Big Roles

In 2002 Johnson also had his first lead movie role in *The Scorpion King*, the prequel to *The Mummy Returns*, which was released in 2001. In *The Mummy Returns* Johnson's character had a smaller role. In *The Scorpion King*, though, Johnson's character, Mathayus, is the lead role. Mathayus, the leader of assassins, is supposed to kill a sorceress who has been using her powers to help the evil Memnon rule most of the world. However, when Mathayus captures the sorceress, he learns that she has not been Memnon's helper, she has been his captive. With the sorceress out of Memnon's clutches, Mathayus is able to rally the leaders of the free tribes and defeat Memnon. The film was financially successful. It grossed $91 million in the United States and $165 million worldwide.

Johnson's next wrestling successes in 2002 were in July, when he defeated both the Undertaker and Kurt Angle to take back the

WWE title. However, he lost the title the next month to Brock Lesnar. Wrestling was taking more and more of a back seat to Johnson's acting roles, though. In fact, in 2003 Johnson took part in only a handful of matches. In February he beat Hulk Hogan in the No Way Out event. His next win was against Steve Austin at WrestleMania XIX on March 30. His winning streak ended, though, when he was defeated by Bill Goldberg on April 27 at Backlash.

In the meantime, Johnson's next movie *The Rundown* was released in July 2002. In this film Johnson played Beck, a repo man who is sent to South America to locate a treasure hunter. Though it had some favorable reviews, the film did not make as much money as *The Scorpion King*. In fact, it grossed just over half as much as the previous film. Despite this, it was another film role to add to his résumé.

The Next Arnold Schwarzenegger

By this time Johnson was being compared to earlier action stars like Arnold Schwarzenegger and Sylvester Stallone. One critic remarked on his performance in *The Rundown*, "For fun and money, this is The Rock's biggest [role]. . . . And this time he scores at more than just the box office."[19] Some critics seemed to be surprised that a wrestler could make such a successful transition into acting. In fact, some of these critics said he was a better actor than some other action stars. It was not such a surprise to Johnson, though, who had used acting skills in the wrestling ring for years.

On March 14, 2004, Johnson entered the ring in WrestleMania XX. In an event billed as the Handicap Match, the Rock and Mick Foley tag-teamed against Ric Flair, Randy Orton, and Batista. The Rock and Foley lost. This was the Rock's last match. It was the end of his wrestling contract, and Johnson was now free to pursue acting without having to split his time with wrestling.

His next movie *Walking Tall* was released in April of that same year. *Walking Tall* was a loosely based remake of a 1973 film. In this movie Johnson played Chris Vaughan, a former member of the U.S. Army Special Forces. Johnson's character returns to his hometown in Washington State after an absence of eight years to

In 2004 Johnson starred in the remake of Walking Tall. *He received favorable reviews and public acclaim for his performance.*

take over his family's business, which he finds has been closed down. He discovers his once-peaceful hometown has been overtaken by drugs and violence, thanks in part to the presence of a crooked gambling casino. Vaughan becomes sheriff and proceeds to clean up his town the hard way, with much violence.

Once again, a number of reviews of Johnson's acting talents was favorable. A reviewer for the Web site Celebritywonder.com wrote,

> Casting-wise this is by far a one-man show for The Rock. Dwayne Johnson, aka "The Rock", has been called the most entertaining man in sports entertainment, and it shows in this film. Despite my reservations of his film project choices, there is no doubting that this man has a presence. You can't help but root for this guy as he's likable and a total hardcore action star.[20]

After appearing in several action films in a row, Johnson made a big change in character types to act in *Be Cool*, the sequel to *Get Shorty*. Released March 4, 2005, this was Johnson's first entirely comic role, which came as a big surprise to his action film fans. In the film, Johnson plays a gay, country-western-singing bodyguard. His job is to protect a talent manager played by Vince Vaughn. Once again Johnson had some favorable reviews. He was described as refreshing and witty, with a talent for comic timing, which brought some of the movie's biggest laughs.

The Rock No More

In a few years' time, Johnson had made the jump from one successful career to another. First, he succeeded as a wrestler on his own, without trading on his father's or his grandfather's career. He had made a success of the Rock, the brash, arrogant character that fans loved to hate. He had also proved that he had talents other than those he had demonstrated so often in the ring. Although he was extremely grateful for all he had gained from his wrestling career, he wanted to keep the Rock, the wrestling character, separate from Dwayne Johnson, the actor. To do this, he planned to phase out the very role that had brought him fame and fortune.

With his full-time transition to acting, Johnson felt it was time to drop the nickname, the Rock. Just as a movie role, the Rock was a role—a character Johnson had played in the ring. The Rock was a character with a personality and attitude separate from that of Dwayne Johnson, and, although he was grateful for the success his wrestling persona had brought him, Johnson no longer wanted to be identified with that character.

In fact, fans and some interviewers appear to have more trouble dropping the name than Johnson has. It still crops up in the titles of articles, and some fans still refer to Johnson as the Rock. Johnson realizes the transition is difficult for some people to make, so he has patiently explained his reasons to a number of interviewers. In a 2007 interview, he explained it this way:

WWE Hall of Fame

In March 2008 Dwayne Johnson's father Rocky Johnson and his grandfather High Chief Peter Maivia were inducted into the WWE Hall of Fame. This institution has been honoring professional wrestlers since 1993, when it was called the WWF Hall of Fame and inducted its first honoree, Andre the Giant. The well-known wrestler had died earlier that year.

Since its beginning, the induction ceremonies have been held in many locations, such as Omni Inner Harbor International Hotel in Baltimore, Maryland, the Hilton in New York City, Universal Amphitheater in Los Angeles, California, and the site of the 2008 ceremony, Amway Arena in Orlando, Florida. Although the WWE Hall of Fame is at present an event rather than an actual location, WWE executives are looking into acquiring a site so they can bring the wrestling memorabilia out of the warehouses, where they have been stored for years. At this time, a site and a construction schedule are still several years in the future.

From now on please call me Dwayne Johnson. I want to be known as Dwayne Johnson the actor, and not The Rock. I loved the Rock; The Rock was a nickname but what happened is it's naturally progressed into Dwayne "The Rock" Johnson. When it becomes just Dwayne Johnson, as it will in the next movie, *Southland Tales*, that's fine. I never wanted to make that defining statement. It just didn't feel right to me.[21]

With the transition back to just plain Dwayne Johnson, he has continued to broaden his acting roles, playing less violent, more comedic roles such as quarterback Joe "the King" Kingman in the comedy film *The Game Plan*. In this film, he plays a hard-living football star who becomes responsible for an eight-year-old daughter, Peyton, he never knew he had. Johnson's character has to change from high-living and all-night partying to seeking out ballet classes, arranging playdates, and reading bedtime stories. In a further shock to Johnson's onetime wrestling fans, his character appears in tights in his daughter's ballet recital. Johnson did not have far to go to research for this role. He just had to draw from his own experiences with his daughter Simone.

Personal Changes

Quite separate from the loud, brash, confrontational role he played as the Rock, Johnson conducts himself with courtesy and dignity. Nowhere is this more evident than in the way he has behaved during his separation and subsequent divorce from his wife Dany, now a successful financial adviser. The two separated in June 2007 after ten years of marriage, and their divorce became final in May 2008. According to announcements made through publicists, the two will share custody of their daughter. Apparently, they have put their daughter's feelings and welfare first throughout this difficult process. For instance, when she is with one parent, she is free to telephone the other parent whenever she likes, and both parents will continue to have major roles in her life as she grows up.

Johnson and his ex-wife also behaved amicably and respectfully to each other during this time. They did not indulge in public accusations and insults that sometimes accompany the divorces of famous people. The two have avoided public battles and spiteful behavior. Whatever personal differences they have they have chosen to keep to themselves. In fact, a number of entertainment reports have remarked that all of Hollywood would do well to follow their example under such circumstances.

The two have apparently maintained a friendly working relationship and plan to continue working together on charity efforts begun during their marriage. Among these are donations to the University of Miami, the Red Cross, and some charitable foundations they personally started.

Philanthropist

For instance, the Johnsons founded the Dwayne Johnson Rock Foundation. This organization was developed to improve self-esteem among young people, promote physical fitness, and provide obesity prevention education, including nutritional counseling. The foundation also helps young people in the United States and in other countries develop and achieve educational goals. Founded in 2006, the Dwayne Johnson Rock Foundation has supported such charities as The Rock's Toy Chest, a corporate sponsorship program designed to supply school supplies, clothing, and other necessities to children in impoverished countries, including El Salvador, Guatemala, and Lesotho.

The foundation also sponsors Project Knapsack. Project Knapsack will be a pen pal and school supply partnership between schoolchildren in the United States and needy children in third-world countries. Through this program, students will be able to share information about their countries, foods, hobbies, climates, and other issues of interest to them. To do this, students in the United States will write letters, which will be placed into the knapsacks with school supplies. The knapsacks will go to students in impoverished countries. Not only will they have supplies they need, they will also have the opportunity to learn about life in another part of the world.

Another of their charitable foundations is Beacon Experience, founded by Dany Johnson. This organization also focuses on the

Johnson signs autographs for fans at the Summer on the Pier event benefiting The Rock Foundation. His foundation supports many charities for children.

welfare of young people, an issue that has always been important to the Johnsons. The mission of Beacon Experience is to motivate disadvantaged students to stay in school and, beyond that, provide the means for them to go to college. The program works by providing volunteers to serve as role models and tutors. The organization sponsors parent meetings, field trips, and other after-school programs.

Johnson's concern for children also led him to become a supporter of the Make-A-Wish Foundation. The Make-A-Wish Foundation grants wishes to children with life-threatening health conditions.

Make-A-Wish Foundation

Many famous people, including wrestler-turned-actor Dwayne Johnson, donate money and time to deserving charities. One charity in which Johnson has been involved is the Make-A-Wish Foundation. The Make-A-Wish Foundation was founded in 1980, and has enriched the lives of children with life-threatening conditions for over two decades.

The Make-A-Wish Foundation began with the wish of one seven-year-old boy, Christopher James Greicius. Christopher had leukemia. He dreamed of becoming a police officer but his family knew that day might never come. U.S. Customs officer Tommy Austin was a family friend. He promised young Christopher a ride in a police helicopter. Austin contacted a friend with the Arizona Department of Public Safety, and together they planned a special day for Christopher. They also had a uniform made just for him. Christopher had his special day, but his condition worsened and he died a few days later.

Since then, the Make-A-Wish foundation has grown to a network of almost 25,000 volunteers, including sponsors, donors, and entire communities. Altogether, the Make-A-Wish Foundation has worked with more than 167,000 ill children between the ages of two-and-a-half and eighteen, by granting their special wishes.

These are some of the positive ways Johnson chooses to use his celebrity status to benefit others. But like hard-working people in any profession, Johnson also cherishes his private time and enjoys activities that have nothing to do with wrestling or making movies. For instance, few people know that Johnson is a very good light tackle, saltwater fisherman. He is also a big fan of the music of Elvis Presley. In fact, Johnson can play guitar and sing. Although he has sung in some of his movies, probably his most appreciative audience to date is his daughter Simone, for whom he plays guitar and sings when they are together.

Future Directions

Johnson's future as an actor appears solid. He has movies in release as well as movies still in production. In fact, even though his days of splitting his time between two careers are long past, he seems to be busier than ever, playing both supporting and leading roles. One movie, *Southland Tales* from Universal Studios, was released late in 2007. Described as both a science-fiction movie and a dark comedy, the story takes place in Los Angeles, California, in an alternate 2008. The United States has undergone some turbulent times. Part of Texas has been wiped out in a nuclear attack, and California is on the brink of environmental and economic collapse. Johnson plays Boxer Santaros, an action film star with amnesia.

Another film, *Get Smart* from Warner Brothers, was released in June 2008. In this film, based on an early television series by the same name, Johnson plays Agent 23, a superstar agent with the government spy agency Control. Following a plot line similar to the television series, the evil crime syndicate KAOS is threatening to take over the world and must be stopped by Control. In a recent interview, Johnson said he had a great time making the movie and that it was a great experience working with such funny material as well as costar Steve Carell, who plays the lead character Maxwell Smart. He also said it was sometimes hard to keep a straight face in some of the scenes. Johnson had been a fan of the original series, which he had watched in reruns as a child.

The 2008 film Get Smart, *based on the 1960s television series, featured Dwayne Johnson (left) and Steve Carell (right). The movie was a huge hit.*

Johnson's responsibilities as a father influence many of his recent role choices, such as Las Vegas cab driver Freddy Hasby in the comedy/action film *Escape to Witch Mountain* by Disney Studios, a remake of a 1975 children's classic. Hasby is hired to drive orphaned twins to a place of safety. Along the way he has to thwart the evil billionaire who wants to kidnap the children and exploit their paranormal powers.

One film project still in developmental stages and close to Johnson's heart is the title role in *King Kamehameha*, a film for Columbia Tri-Star Studios. The great Hawaiian king united and ruled several tribal islands from 1795 to 1819. Though some Polynesians question an actor of Samoan descent playing this role, some historians argue that Kamehameha actually descended from Samoans. There is as yet no word on a production schedule or release date for this tentative project.

Although Johnson left wrestling to become an actor, he has not completely turned away from the career that made him famous. He still occasionally appears at wrestling events as a guest, not a performer. On Saturday, March 29, 2008, at the Amway Arena in Orlando, Florida, Johnson inducted his father Rocky Johnson and his grandfather High Chief Peter Maivia into the WWE Hall of Fame.

Honoring Stunt Men and Women

In April 2007 Dwayne Johnson hosted the 2007 Taurus World Stunt Awards. This is the entertainment industry's only such program to honor the top stunt professionals. Johnson had also hosted the program in 2005. As an action movie star, Johnson has had many opportunities to watch stunt men and women perform their remarkable feats. He spoke of his admiration for the people in this profession: "I have the utmost respect for the stunt community, which is why I am so happy to be hosting the TWSA for the second time. As actors, we truly appreciate all that they do as they literally put their lives on the line for the sake of filmmaking. The stunt community is like family to me and I'm proud to be a part of honoring them."

Taurus World Stunt Awards, "Dwayne The Rock Johnson to Host 2007 Taurus World Stunt Awards," press release, April 18, 2007. www.taurusworldstuntawards.com/index.php?cmd=cmdnewsletterdetail&id=8.

As for the future, Johnson will continue to make films and share business and child-raising responsibilities with his ex-wife. He admits to being rocked to his core by scandals and tragedies in the wrestling business, including the Chris Benoit murder/suicide, and he adamantly advocates for a zero tolerance policy in the sport of wrestling regarding steroid use. He has also expressed some aspiration toward a political career. Because he has already been successful in two out of three careers, the odds may be in his favor if he chooses to step into that ring.

Chapter 1: A Royal Family and Rocky Roads

1. Dwayne Johnson with Joe Layden, *The Rock Says . . . : The Most Electrifying Man in Sports Entertainment*. New York: HarperCollins, 1999, p. 15.
2. Quoted in Dan Ross, *The Story of the Wrestler They Call "The Rock."* Philadelphia: Chelsea House, 2000, p. 17.
3. Johnson, *The Rock Says . . .* , p. 21.
4. Johnson, *The Rock Says . . .* , p. 45.
5. Quoted in Jacqueline Laks Gorman, *Dwayne "The Rock" Johnson*. Pleasantville, NY: Gareth Stevens, 2008, p. 15.

Chapter 2: Joining the Family Business

6. Quoted in indieLondon, "The Game Plan—Dwayne 'The Rock' Johnson Interview." March 5, 2008. www.indielondon. co.uk/Film-Review/the-game-plan-dwayne-the-rock-johnson-interview.
7. Quoted in The Wrestling Gospel According to Mike Mooneyham, "The Rock" Cooking Up Titles, 1998. www. mikemooneyham.com/pages/viewfull.cfm?ObjectID=67F95 9AF-EBBE-4187-843CDF90AAC4707E=EBBE-4187-843C DF90AAC4707E.
8. Johnson, *The Rock Says . . .* , p. 138.
9. Johnson, *The Rock Says . . .* , pp. 138–39.

Chapter 3: Making His Name

10. Johnson, *The Rock Says . . .* , p. 160.

Chapter 4: Introducing the Rock

11. Johnson, *The Rock Says . . .* , p. 161.
12. Quoted in Ross, *The Story of the Wrestler They Call The Rock*, p. 41.
13. Quoted in ImpeccableDwayneJohnson.net.http://impecca bledwaynejohnson.net/main1/pages/quotes/.

14. Quoted in Ross, *The Story of the Wrestler They Call The Rock*, pp. 42–43.
15. Quoted in Ross, *The Story of the Wrestler They Call The Rock*, p. 45.
16. Quoted in CNN.com, "Wrestler Owen Hart Killed in Fall During Stunt." www.cnn.com/US/9905/24/wrestler.dies04/index.html.
17. Quoted in the Insider, "Johnson Is Whipped by His Daughter." www.dotspotter.com/news/371193_Dwayne_Johnson_is_Whipped_by_his_daughter.
18. Quoted in Gamespot. http://videogames.yahoo.com/celebrity-byte/dwayne-the-rock-johnson/532302/2.

Chapter 5: Knowing Your Roles

19. Michael Wilmington, Chicago Metromix, "Movie Review: The Rundown." Chicagometromix.com/movies/reviewmovie-review-the-rundown/158534/content.
20. Mark McCloud, "Movie Reviews," Celebritywonder.com. www.celebritywonder.com/movie/2004_Walking Tall.html
21. Quoted in contactmusic.com, "Don't Call Me The Rock." www.contactmusic.com/news.nsf/article/johnson%20dont%20call%20me%20the%20rock_1007912.

1972

On May 2 Dwayne Douglas Johnson is born in Hayward, California.

1991

Johnson begins college and joins the football team at the University of Miami.

1995

Johnson graduates from the University of Miami and has a brief season with the Calgary Stampeders, a franchise in the Canadian Football League.

1996

As Flex Kavana, Johnson's professional wrestling debut with the USWA occurs in June in Cookeville, Tennessee. In November he debuts as Rocky Maivia with the WWF at Madison Square Garden, New York City.

1997

Wins first WWF title from Hunter Hearst Helmsley on February 13. Loses title to Owen Hart on April 12. Marries Dany Garcia on May 3. Turns heel and becomes the Rock. Joins Nation of Domination, a wrestling faction led by Faarooq.

1998

Takes over Nation of Domination from Faarooq. In November. he wins WWF World title in the Survivor Series by beating Mankind. On December 29 he loses World title to Mankind.

1999

WWF World title passes back and forth between the Rock, Mankind, and Steve Austin. Writes autobiography *The Rock Says . . . The Most Electrifying Man in Sports Entertainment*.

2000

The Rock Says . . . tops the *New York Times* best-seller list in January. Backlash beats Triple H to take back the WWF title in April. King of the Ring six-man tag-team match in June; the Rock, Kane, and the Undertaker win WWF Tag Team title.

2001

Release of the movie *The Mummy Returns* with Johnson playing the Scorpion King. He splits his time between making movies and his wrestling career.

2002

Johnson has lead role in *The Scorpion King*. Begins cutting back on number of wrestling matches. In July he beats the Undertaker and Kurt Angle in the Vengeance series to take the WWE title.

2003

The movie *The Rundown* is released in September.

2004

Last professional match, WrestleMania XX, in March. *Walking Tall* released in April.

2005

Be Cool released in April, *Doom* in October.

2006

Gridiron Gang released in September.

2007

Dwayne and Dany Johnson announce their separation. *Southland Tales* released.

2008

In March Johnson inducts his father Rocky Johnson and his late grandfather High Chief Peter Maivia into the WWE Hall of Fame. The Johnsons' divorce becomes final in May. *Get Smart* released in June.

Books

Jacqueline Laks Gorman, *Dwayne "The Rock" Johnson*. Pleasantville, NY: Gareth Stevens, 2008. Although a biography for younger readers, this book contains a surprising number of details about the private life and careers of Dwayne Johnson.

Dwayne Johnson with Joe Layden, *The Rock Says . . . : The Most Electrifying Man in Sports Entertainment*. New York: Harper-Collins, 1999. Although more appropriate for older readers due to some adult language and situations, this is a comprehensive and enlightening first-person work.

Don Ross, *The Story of the Wrestler They Call "The Rock."* A brief but comprehensive biography focusing on the wrestling career of Dwayne "the Rock" Johnson. Narrated in "angle," or storyline language.

Web Sites

DJ Rock Foundation (www.djrockfoundation.org). This site contains information on Dwayne and Dany Johnson's charities for children.

Dwayne Johnson Fever (www.dwaynejohnsonfever.net). This is a fan source dedicated to former professional wrestler and actor Dwayne "the Rock" Johnson. It includes a brief biography, trivia, interview, photos, and information on upcoming appearances.

Gary Will's Wrestling History (www.garywill.com/wrestling). This site provides links to a variety of sites and articles about the history of professional wrestling.

Impeccable Dwayne Johnson (www.impeccabledwaynejohnson.net/main1/). This fan source includes the latest headlines about Dwayne Johnson, an article archive, filmography, and a registered forum.

World Wrestling Entertainment (www.wwe.com). This official Web site of the WWE includes information on WWE stars, pay-per-view schedules, and upcoming events. Also includes a "store" where fans can order T-shirts and other WWE memorabilia.

A

Angle, Kurt, 79

Anoa'i, Afa, 17

Anoa'i, Sika, 17

Anoa'i wrestling family,
  18

Atlas, Tony, 16

Austin, Stone Cold Steve,
  61, 80

B

Be Cool (film), 82

Beacon Experience, 85, 87

Benoit, Chris, 67

Booker T, 79

Bravo, Dina, 71

C

Canadian Football League,
  28

Carell, Steve, 88

The Corporation, 68

D

Dundee, Bill, 42

E

Eric, Fritz Von, 39

Escape to Witch Mountain
  (film), 89

F

Faarooq. *See* Simmons, Ron
  "Faarooq"

Foley, Mick, 75, 80

Funk, Terry, 16

G

The Game Plan (film), 84

Garcia, Dany. *See* Johnson,
  Dany Garcia

Get Shorty (film), 82

Get Smart (film), 88, *89*

Goldberg, Bill, 80

Goodish, Frank "Bruiser
  Brody," 71

Guerrero, Eddie, 71

Gunn, Billy, 75

H

Hart, Bret, 52

Hart, Owen, 43, *44*, 71
  death of, 72, *73*, 74

Haskins, David, 43

Hawk, Road Warrior, 71

Helmsley, Hunter Hearst, 50

Hernandez, Hercules, 71

Highspot, 55

Hogan, Hulk, 80

J

Jarrett, Jeff, 39, 40

Jericho, Chris, 79

Johnson, Ata (mother), 14

Johnson, Dany Garcia
  (wife), 25, 29, 56–57, 70
  with Dwayne, *26, 30*

Johnson, Dwayne, *11, 24,*
  51, 65, 69, 86
  in 1992 Orange Bowl, 27
  as actor, 75
  becomes "the Rock,"
    61–63
  with Calgary Stampeders,
    27–28
  with Dany Garcia, *26, 30*
  debut at Madison Square
    Garden, *48, 49*
  early life of, 18–21
  ends wrestling career, 80
  feud with Austin, 63–64,
    66
  as Flex Kavana, 42–45
  in *Get Smart,* 89
  on his grandfather, 17
  with his mother, *14*
  with Jerry Lawler, *41*

marries Dany Garcia, 57

in *The Mummy Returns, 76*

as parent, 76

recruited by college
  football teams, 21

in the ring, *33, 53*

as a role model, 70

in *The Scorpion King, 78*

signs first wrestling
  contract, 39

with Stone Cold Steve
  Austin, 62

trains for wrestling career,
  32, 34

at University of Miami,
  22–23, 25

in *Walking Tall, 81*

WWF debut of, 7

Johnson, Rocky "Soulman"
  (father), 10
  comments on son, 14, 16,
    31
  inducted into WWE Hall
    of Fame, 83, 90

Johnson, Simone Alexandra
  (daughter), 9, 75

Jonathan, Don Leo, 16

K

Kavana, Flex. *See* Johnson,
  Dwayne

King Kamehameha (film), 90

L
Lawler, Jerry, 39, 40, 41
Lesnar, Brock, 80
Levesque, Paul Michael, 50
Lombardi, Steve, 36
The Long Shot (film), 75

M
Madison Square Garden, 47, 48, 49
Maivia, Fanene Leifi Pita (grandfather), 10, 12–14, 17, 18
inducted into WWF Hall of Fame, 83, 90
Make-a-Wish Foundation, 87
Matsuda, Hiro, 58
McMahon, Linda, 74
McMahon, Vince, 37, 38, 63
Mero, Marc, 49
Miami Hurricanes, 23
The Mummy Returns (film), 75

N
Nation of Domination, 58, 59, 60

No-show, 55–56

P
Patterson, Pat, 13, 34, 35

R
Race, Harley, 16
Roberts, Jake, 49
The Rock Says... (Dwayne Johnson), 75
The Rundown (film), 80

S
Samoan culture, 12
Saturday Night Live (TV program), 75, 77, 79
The Scorpion King (film), 8, 80
Shamrock, Ken, 66–67
Simmons, Ron "Faarooq," 58, 67–68
Smith, Davey Boy, 71
Southland Tales (film), 88

T
Taurus World Stunt Awards, 90
Tolos, John, 16

U
United States Wrestling Alliance (USWA), 39–40

W

Walking Tall (film), 80, *81*, 82

Windham, Barry, 49

World Wrestling
  Entertainment, Inc.
  (WWE), 74

World Wrestling
  Entertainment Hall of
  Fame, 83

World Wrestling Federation
  (WWF)

becomes World Wrestling
  Entertainment, Inc., 74

Dwayne joins, 46–47, 49

Dwayne's first tryout with,
  36–37

wrestling, 15

deaths in, 71

drug problems in, 67

meaning of "baby-face" in,
  52

showmanship in, 54–55

Sheila Wyborny, a retired teacher, has been writing nonfiction titles for children and young adults for almost ten years. She and her husband, a consulting engineer and pilot, live on a community airport near Houston, Texas. When time permits, Wyborny packs her portable office and travels with her husband.